DALLAS
SHOPPING

RECOMMENDED STORES FOR VISITORS

The Most Positively Reviewed and Recommended Stores in the City

EGP
Editorial

DALLAS SHOPPING GUIDE 2022
Best Rated Stores in Dallas, Texas

© Winston B. Abbott
© E.G.P. Editorial

ISBN-13: 9798504887203

DALLAS SHOPPING GUIDE

Most Recommended Stores in the City

*This directory is dedicated to the Business Owners and Managers
who provide the experience that the locals and tourists enjoy.
Thanks you very much for all that you do and thank for being the "People Choice".*

*Thanks to everyone that posts their reviews online and
the amazing reviews sites that make our life easier.*

*The places listed in this book are the most positively reviewed
and recommended by locals and travelers from around the world.*

*Thank you for your time and enjoy the directory that is
designed with locals and tourist in mind!*

TOP 500
SHOPPING SPOTS

The Most Recommended
(from #1 to #500)

#1
The Quadrangle
Category: Shopping Centers
Average Price: Expensive
Area: Uptown
Address: 2828 Routh St
Dallas, TX 75201
Phone: (214) 220-3709

#2
Galleria Dallas
Category: Shopping Centers
Average Price: Expensive
Area: North Dallas
Address: 13350 Dallas Pkwy
Dallas, TX 75240
Phone: (972) 702-7100

#3
The Shops At Park Lane
Category: Shopping Centers
Average Price: Modest
Area: Lake Highlands
Address: 8080 Park Ln
Dallas, TX 75231
Phone: (214) 365-0222

#4
Davis Street Mercantile
Category: Home Decor, Gift Shops,
Women's Clothing
Average Price: Modest
Area: Oak Cliff
Address: 710 West Davis St
Dallas, TX 75208
Phone: (214) 541-9999

#5
Northpark Center
Category: Shopping Centers
Average Price: Expensive
Area: North Dallas
Address: 8687 N Central Expy
Dallas, TX 75225
Phone: (214) 363-7441

#6
Westend Market Place
Category: Shopping Centers
Average Price: Exclusive
Area: West End, Downtown
Address: 603 Munger Ave
Dallas, TX 75202
Phone: (214) 303-0107

#7
Village On The Parkway
Category: Shopping Centers
Average Price: Modest
Area: Addison
Address: 5100 Belt Line Rd
Dallas, TX 75254
Phone: (972) 308-0100

#8
Favor The Kind
Category: Home Decor, Women's Clothing
Average Price: Expensive
Area: Lower Greenville
Address: 2928 N Henderson Ave
Dallas, TX 75206
Phone: (214) 370-8010

#9
We Are 1976
Category: Gift Shops, Art Galleries,
Printing Services
Average Price: Modest
Area: Bishop Arts District, Oak Cliff
Address: 313 N Bishop Ave
Dallas, TX 75208
Phone: (214) 821-1976

#10
Fête-Ish
Category: Accessories, Home Decor
Average Price: Modest
Area: Bishop Arts District, Oak Cliff
Address: 322 W 7th St
Dallas, TX 75208
Phone: (214) 948-9874

#11
Kettledrum Allie Boutique
Category: Women's Clothing, Accessories
Average Price: Modest
Area: Bishop Arts District, Oak Cliff
Address: 509 N Bishop St
Dallas, TX 75208
Phone: (214) 535-6441

#12
Jade & Clover
Category: Accessories,
Home Decor, Gift Shops
Average Price: Modest
Area: Deep Ellum
Address: 2633 Main St
Dallas, TX 75226
Phone: (469) 730-2264

#13
Deep Ellum Outdoor Market
Category: Flea Markets
Average Price: Modest
Area: Deep Ellum
Address: 2636 Main St
Dallas, TX 75226
Phone: (214) 785-8295

#14
Out Of The Closet - Dallas
Category: Vintage & Consignment
Average Price: Inexpensive
Area: Oak Lawn
Address: 3920 Cedar Springs Rd.
Dallas, TX 75219
Phone: (214) 599-2173

#15
Life Of Riley
Category: Gift Shops,
Average Price: Modest
Area: Deep Ellum
Address: 2814 Main St
Dallas, TX 75226
Phone: (214) 749-0509

#16
Dallas Pinup
Category: Women's Clothing, Photography
Stores & Services, Accessories
Average Price: Modest
Area: Deep Ellum
Address: 2928 Main St
Dallas, TX 75226
Phone: (214) 741-4206

#17
Strut
Category: Women's Clothing
Average Price: Modest
Area: Bishop Arts District, Oak Cliff
Address: 408 N Bishop Ave
Dallas, TX 75208
Phone: (214) 942-1090

#18
Bullzerk
Category: Screen Printing/T-Shirt Printing,
Men's Clothing, Women's Clothing
Average Price: Inexpensive
Area: Lower Greenville
Address: 1909 Greenville Ave
Dallas, TX 75206
Phone: (972) 677-7705

#19
Victory Park
Category: Shopping Centers
Average Price: Inexpensive
Area: Victory Park
Address: 2323 Victory Ave
Dallas, TX 75219
Phone: (972) 663-9600

#20
Nordstrom Rack
Category: Women's Clothing,
Shoe Stores
Average Price: Modest
Area: North Dallas
Address: 13900 Dallas Pkwy
Dallas, TX 75240
Phone: (214) 234-2808

#21
My Secret Closet
Category: Women's Clothing
Average Price: Modest
Area: North Dallas
Address: 17390 Preston Rd
Dallas, TX 75252
Phone: (972) 267-1144

#22
Tenoversix
Category: Women's Clothing,
Men's Clothing
Average Price: Expensive
Area: Downtown
Address: 1511 Commerce St
Dallas, TX 75201
Phone: (214) 261-4540

#23
Kiss Bartique
Category: Women's Clothing
Average Price: Modest
Area: West End, Downtown
Address: 1701 N Market St
Dallas, TX 75202
Phone: (214) 939-1000

#24
Neighborhood
Category: Cards & Stationery, Furniture
Stores, Home Decor
Average Price: Modest
Area: Bishop Arts District, Oak Cliff
Address: 411 N Bishop
Dallas, TX 75208
Phone: (214) 943-5650

#25
Clotheshorse Anonymous
Category: Women's Clothing, Used, Vintage & Consignment, Accessories
Average Price: Modest
Area: North Dallas
Address: 11661 Preston Rd
Dallas, TX 75230
Phone: (972) 233-7005

#26
Dd's DISCOUNTS
Category: Discount Store, Women's Clothing, Home Decor
Average Price: Modest
Area: North Dallas
Address: 10020 Marsh Ln
Dallas, TX 75229
Phone: (214) 353-9355

#27
Neiman Marcus
Category: Men's Clothing
Average Price: Exclusive
Area: Downtown
Address: 1618 Main St
Dallas, TX 75201
Phone: (214) 741-6911

#28
Lula B's
Category: Used, Vintage & Consignment
Average Price: Modest
Area: Oak Cliff
Address: 1982 Fort Worth Ave
Dallas, TX 75208
Phone: (214) 824-2185

#29
Guns And Roses Boutique
Category: Women's Clothing, Men's Clothing
Average Price: Modest
Area: Downtown
Address: 2014 Commerce St
Dallas, TX 75201
Phone: (214) 748-7673

#30
Zara
Category: Men's Clothing, Women's Clothing
Average Price: Modest
Area: Downtown
Address: 13350 Dallas Pkwy
Dallas, TX 75295
Phone: (972) 392-0622

#31
The Junky Monkey's So Posh
Category: Used, Vintage & Consignment
Average Price: Modest
Area: Lower Greenville
Address: 2400 N Henderson Ave
Dallas, TX 75206
Phone: (214) 477-3427

#33
Opportunity Market
Category: Women's Clothing, Gift Shops
Average Price: Modest
Area: Bishop Arts District, Oak Cliff
Address: 415 N Bishop Ave
Dallas, TX 75208
Phone: (877) 564-3247

#32
B4
Category: Used, Vintage & Consignment
Average Price: Modest
Area: Deep Ellum
Address: 2707 Main St
Dallas, TX 75226
Phone: (214) 923-4983

#34
Silver Moon Factory
Category: Jewelry, Women's Clothing
Average Price: Modest
Area: North Dallas
Address: 11538 Harry Hines Blvd
Dallas, TX 75229
Phone: (972) 247-7511

#35
Read Between The Lines
Category: Gift Shops, Cards & Stationery
Average Price: Modest
Area: Victory Park
Address: 2412 Victory Park Ln
Dallas, TX 75219
Phone: (469) 904-8034

#36
Bishop Street Market
Category: Cards & Stationery, Accessories
Average Price: Modest
Area: Bishop Arts District, Oak Cliff
Address: 419 N Bishop Ave
Dallas, TX 75208
Phone: (214) 941-0907

#37
Uncommon Market Inc
Category: Antiques, Home
Decor, Furniture Stores
Average Price: Expensive
Area: Design District
Address: 100 Riveredge Dr
Dallas, TX 75207
Phone: (214) 871-2775

#38
Mockingbird Commons
Category: Shopping Centers
Average Price: Modest
Area: Lakewood
Address: 6333 E Mockingbird Ln
Dallas, TX 75214
Phone: (214) 706-2502

#39
Pitaya
Category: Accessories, Women's Clothing
Average Price: Modest
Area: Uptown
Address: 3699 Mckinney Ave
Dallas, TX 75204
Phone: (214) 252-9700

#40
Pennies For Heaven Resale
Category: Thrift Stores, Used,
Vintage & Consignment
Average Price: Modest
Area: North Dallas
Address: 17471 Preston Rd
Dallas, TX 75252
Phone: (972) 982-2726

#41
T J Maxx
Category: Department Stores
Average Price: Modest
Area: North Dallas
Address: 14754 Preston Rd
Dallas, TX 75254
Phone: (972) 702-8535

#42
Nordstrom Rack
Category: Women's Clothing, Shoe Stores,
Department Stores
Average Price: Modest
Area: Lake Highlands
Address: 8050 Park Ln
Dallas, TX 75231
Phone: (214) 932-6222

#43
Betty Lou
Category: Fashion
Average Price: Modest
Area: Uptown
Address: 3207 Knox St
Dallas, TX 75205
Phone: (214) 206-9514

#44
Stanley Korshak
Category: Department Stores, Men's
Clothing, Women's Clothing
Average Price: Exclusive
Area: Uptown
Address: 500 Crescent Ct
Dallas, TX 75201
Phone: (214) 871-3600

#45
Traffic La At The Joule
Category: Women's Clothing,
Men's Clothing, Accessories
Average Price: Exclusive
Area: Downtown
Address: 1608 Main St
Dallas, TX 75201
Phone: (214) 261-4585

#46
DLM Supply
Category: Men's Clothing, Accessories
Average Price: Expensive
Area: Oak Cliff
Address: 837 W Davis St
Dallas, TX 75208
Phone: (469) 917-8081

#47
Y&I Clothing Boutique
Category: Women's Clothing,
Accessories, Shoe Stores
Average Price: Modest
Area: Uptown
Address: 3699 Mckinney Ave
Dallas, TX 75204
Phone: (214) 522-0775

#48
Untuckit
Category: Men's Clothing, Women's Clothing
Average Price: Modest
Area: Uptown
Address: 3699 Mckinney Ave
Dallas, TX 75204
Phone: (469) 608-8045

#49
Gypsy House
Category: Women's Clothing,
Accessories, Jewelry
Average Price: Modest
Area: Oak Cliff
Address: 421 N Tyler St
Dallas, TX 75208
Phone: (214) 943-9335

#50
Planet Blue Dallas
Category: Women's Clothing,
Swimwear, Accessories
Average Price: Expensive
Area: Lower Greenville
Address: 3010 N Henderson Ave
Dallas, TX 75206
Phone: (972) 925-0304

#51
On Consignment
Category: Vintage & Consignment
Average Price: Modest
Area: Uptown
Address: 2719 Fairmount St
Dallas, TX 75201
Phone: (214) 720-1818

#52
Wild Bill's Western Store
Category: Fashion, Customized Merchandise
Average Price: Modest
Area: West End, Downtown
Address: 311 N Market
Dallas, TX 75202
Phone: (214) 954-1050

#53
Society
Category: Candle Stores
Average Price: Modest
Area: Bishop Arts District, Oak Cliff
Address: 403 N Bishop Ave
Dallas, TX 75208
Phone: (214) 942-4600

#54
Plaza Latina Bazzar
Category: Shopping Centers
Average Price: Modest
Area: North Dallas
Address: 11200 Harry Hines Blvd
Dallas, TX 75229
Phone: (972) 241-2710

#55
Tuesday Morning
Category: Department Stores
Average Price: Modest
Area: Addison
Address: 4404 S Beltwood Pkwy
Dallas, TX 75244
Phone: (972) 980-1798

#56
The Loveliest
Category: Embroidery & Crochet,
Home Decor, Gift Shops
Average Price: Modest
Area: Uptown
Address: 2417 Mahon St
Dallas, TX 75201
Phone: (214) 484-7376

#57
Forty Five Ten
Category: Men's Clothing,
Women's Clothing, Jewelry
Average Price: Exclusive
Area: Downtown
Address: 1615 Main St
Dallas, TX 75201
Phone: (214) 559-4510

#58
Curiosities
Category: Antiques
Average Price: Modest
Area: Lakewood
Address: 2025 Abrams Rd
Dallas, TX 75214
Phone: (214) 828-1886

#59
Homegoods
Category: Department Stores, Home Decor
Average Price: Modest
Area: Lake Highlands
Address: 8188 Park Ln
Dallas, TX 75231
Phone: (469) 232-9000

#60
Outlines Menswear
Category: Sports Wear, Men's Clothing
Average Price: Expensive
Area: Oak Lawn
Address: 3906 Cedar Springs Rd
Dallas, TX 75219
Phone: (214) 528-1955

#61
Indigo 1745
Category: Men's Clothing, Women's Clothing
Average Price: Expensive
Area: Bishop Arts District, Oak Cliff
Address: 370 W 7th St
Dallas, TX 75208
Phone: (214) 948-1745

#62
Design District Market
Category: Flea Markets
Average Price: Inexpensive
Area: Design District
Address: 1530 Inspiration Dr
Dallas, TX 75207
Phone: (214) 883-9982

#63
Flirt Boutique
Category: Women's Clothing,
Accessories, Shoe Stores
Average Price: Modest
Area: Uptown
Address: 3699 Mckinney Ave
Dallas, TX 75204
Phone: (214) 754-7001

#64
Vintage Martini
Category: Used, Vintage & Consignment
Average Price: Expensive
Area: Lower Greenville
Address: 2923 N Henderson Ave
Dallas, TX 75206
Phone: (469) 334-0584

#65
Ross Dress For Less
Category: Department Stores, Women's
Clothing, Home Decor
Average Price: Inexpensive
Area: North Dallas
Address: 11888 Marsh Ln
Dallas, TX 75234
Phone: (972) 484-5516

#66
Saint Bernard Outlet
Category: Sporting Goods,
Accessories, Shoe Stores
Average Price: Modest
Area: Lake Highlands
Address: 8044 Park Ln
Dallas, TX 75231
Phone: (214) 758-0429

#67
S E T & C O.
Category: Kitchen & Bath, Home Decor
Average Price: Exclusive
Area: Oak Cliff
Address: 841 W Davis St
Dallas, TX 75208
Phone: (214) 948-1000

#68
Tinka's Designer Resale Clothing
Category: Accessories, Women's Clothing,
Used, Vintage & Consignment
Average Price: Modest
Area: North Dallas
Address: 142 Spring Creek Vlg
Dallas, TX 75248
Phone: (972) 716-9944

#69
Shopseptember
Category: Women's Clothing,
Jewelry, Accessories
Average Price: Modest
Area: Uptown
Address: 3699 Mckinney Ave
Dallas, TX 75204
Phone: (469) 930-8008

#70
Tuesday Morning
Category: Gift Shops
Average Price: Modest
Area: Lake Highlands
Address: 10233 E Northwest Hwy
Dallas, TX 75238
Phone: (214) 343-6056

#71
Versace
Category: Leather Goods, Men's Clothing,
Women's Clothing
Average Price: Exclusive
Area: North Dallas
Address: 8687 N. Central Expsswy
Dallas, TX 75225
Phone: (972) 591-5730

#72
Blue Dahlia
Category: Men's Clothing, Women's Clothing
Average Price: Expensive
Area: Bishop Arts District, Oak Cliff
Address: 414 N Bishop Ave
Dallas, TX 75208
Phone: (214) 943-1275

#73
Sam Moon - Dallas
Category: Jewelry, Accessories, Shoe Stores
Average Price: Inexpensive
Area: Farmer's Branch
Address: 11826 Harry Hines Blvd
Dallas, TX 75234
Phone: (972) 484-3084

#74
Home On Bishop
Category: Jewelry, Home Decor, Accessories
Average Price: Modest
Area: Bishop Arts District, Oak Cliff
Address: 502 N Bishop Ave
Dallas, TX 75208
Phone: (214) 434-1421

#75
Guggenhome
Category: Furniture Stores, Home Decor
Average Price: Modest
Area: Design District
Address: 1426 N Riverfront Blvd
Dallas, TX 75207
Phone: (972) 807-9255

#76
The Laughing Willow
Category: Women's Clothing, Accessories
Average Price: Modest
Area: Bishop Arts District, Oak Cliff
Address: 301 N Bishop Ave
Dallas, TX 75208
Phone: (972) 849-9764

#77
House Of Macgregor
Category: Accessories
Average Price: Modest
Area: Oak Cliff
Address: 614 Davis St , Ste 203
Dallas, TX 75208
Phone: (214) 942-1966

#78
Ross Dress For Less
Category: Home Decor, Women's Clothing,
Department Stores
Average Price: Inexpensive
Area: North Dallas
Address: 16641 Coit Rd
Dallas, TX 75248
Phone: (972) 733-3557

#79
Est. 1914
Category: Women's Clothing, Men's Clothing,
Used, Vintage & Consignment
Average Price: Modest
Area: Oak Cliff
Address: 1325 W Davis St
Dallas, TX 75208
Phone: (972) 925-0984

#80
Walmart Supercenter
Category: Grocery, Department Stores
Average Price: Inexpensive
Area: South Dallas
Address: 200 Short St
Dallas, TX 75232
Phone: (972) 232-6400

#81
Lula B's West
Category: Used, Antiques, Home Decor
Average Price: Modest
Area: Design District
Address: 1010 N Riverfront Blvd
Dallas, TX 75207
Phone: (214) 749-1929

#82
LF
Category: Women's Clothing
Average Price: Expensive
Area: Uptown
Address: 3699 Mckinney Ave
Dallas, TX 75204
Phone: (214) 252-1500

#83
Galleria North
Category: Shopping Centers
Average Price: Modest
Area: North Dallas
Address: 13727 Noel Rd
Dallas, TX 75240
Phone: (972) 716-2908

#84
Marshalls
Category: Department Stores
Average Price: Modest
Area: Oak Cliff
Address: 3434 W Illinois Ave
Dallas, TX 75211
Phone: (214) 331-1300

#85
Hillside Village Shopping Center
Category: Shopping Centers
Average Price: Modest
Area: Lakewood
Address: 6465 E Mockingbird Ln
Dallas, TX 75214
Phone: (214) 989-4155

#86
Genesis Benefit Thrift Store
Category: Used, Vintage & Consignment,
Community Service/Non-Profit, Thrift Stores
Average Price: Inexpensive
Area: Oak Lawn
Address: 3419 Knight St
Dallas, TX 75219
Phone: (214) 520-6644

#87
TJ Maxx
Category: Department Stores
Average Price: Modest
Area: Lake Highlands
Address: 9100 N Central Expy
Dallas, TX 75231
Phone: (214) 373-7310

#88
Marshalls
Category: Department Stores
Average Price: Modest
Area: North Dallas
Address: 3616 Forest Ln
Dallas, TX 75234
Phone: (214) 350-8373

#89
Second Ave Thrift Store
Category: Thrift Stores
Average Price: Modest
Area: South Dallas
Address: 4519 S 2nd Ave
Dallas, TX 75210
Phone: (214) 428-3156

#90
Urban Relics
Category: Thrift Stores, Used,
Vintage & Consignment
Average Price: Modest
Area: East Dallas
Address: 3927 Main St
Dallas, TX 75226
Phone: (214) 827-3927

#91
Accessory Junkie
Category: Accessories, Women's Clothing
Average Price: Modest
Area: Deep Ellum
Address: 3101 Commerce St
Dallas, TX 75226
Phone: (214) 986-8951

#92
Retro Revolution
Category: Accessories, Head Shops
Average Price: Modest
Area: Upper Greenville
Address: 5429 Greenville Ave
Dallas, TX 75206
Phone: (214) 365-9420

#93
Rebekah Fashion
Category: Women's Clothing, Accessories
Average Price: Modest
Area: Farmer's Branch
Address: 11818 Harry Hines Blvd
Dallas, TX 75234
Phone: (972) 481-1751

#94
Deep Vellum Books
Category: Bookstores
Average Price: Modest
Area: Deep Ellum
Address: 3000 Commerce St
Dallas, TX 75226
Phone: (972) 638-7741

#95
Consignment Heaven
Category: Antiques, Used,
Vintage & Consignment
Average Price: Modest
Area: Lower Greenville
Address: 2901 N Henderson Ave
Dallas, TX 75206
Phone: (214) 823-4100

#96
Boxlunch
Category: Men's Clothing,
Women's Clothing, Gift Shops
Average Price: Modest
Area: North Dallas
Address: 13350 Dallas Pkwy.
Dallas, TX 75240
Phone: (972) 361-0025

#97
Epiphany Boutique
Category: Women's Clothing,
Men's Clothing, Accessories
Average Price: Expensive
Area: Bishop Arts District, Oak Cliff
Address: 412 N Bishop Ave
Dallas, TX 75208
Phone: (214) 946-4411

#98
DEMERARA
Category: Men's Clothing, Women's Clothing
Average Price: Expensive
Area: Uptown
Address: 3699 Mckinney Ave
Dallas, TX 75204
Phone: (214) 295-7622

#99
Dd's DISCOUNTS
Category: Discount Store, Women's Clothing
Average Price: Inexpensive
Area: Lake Highlands
Address: 6301 Abrams Rd
Dallas, TX 75231
Phone: (214) 341-1057

#100
Dd's DISCOUNTS
Category: Discount Store,
Women's Clothing, Home Decor
Average Price: Inexpensive
Area: Oak Cliff
Address: 2515 W Jefferson Blvd
Dallas, TX 75211
Phone: (214) 948-3000

#101
Ceylon Et Cie
Category: Home Decor
Average Price: Modest
Area: Design District
Address: 1319 Dragon St
Dallas, TX 75207
Phone: (214) 742-7632

#102
HD's Clothing Company
Category: Men's Clothing
Average Price: Expensive
Area: Lower Greenville
Address: 3018 Greenville Ave
Dallas, TX 75206
Phone: (214) 821-5255

#103
The Store In Lake Highlands
Category: Gift Shops
Average Price: Modest
Area: Lake Highlands
Address: 10233 E Northwest Hwy
Dallas, TX 75238
Phone: (214) 553-8850

#104
Grange Hall
Category: Home Decor, Jewelry, Accessories
Average Price: Exclusive
Area: Uptown
Address: 4445 Travis St
Dallas, TX 75205
Phone: (214) 443-0600

#105
Melrose
Category: Accessories, Women's Clothing
Average Price: Inexpensive
Area: Oak Cliff
Address: 655 W Illinois Ave
Dallas, TX 75201
Phone: (214) 948-5511

#106
**Wynnewood Village
Shopping Center**
Category: Shopping Centers
Average Price: Modest
Area: Oak Cliff
Address: 655 W Illinois Ave
Dallas, TX 75224
Phone: (214) 943-4351

#107
Rally House Old Town
Category: Accessories, Men's Clothing,
Women's Clothing
Average Price: Modest
Area: Upper Greenville
Address: 5500 Greenville Ave
Dallas, TX 75206
Phone: (214) 308-0800

#108
Club Monaco Dallas West Village
Category: Women's Clothing
Average Price: Expensive
Area: Uptown
Address: 3699 Mckinney Ave
Dallas, TX 75204
Phone: (214) 219-2301

#109
Walmart Supercenter
Category: Department Stores
Average Price: Modest
Area: North Dallas
Address: 4122 Lyndon B Johnson Fwy
Dallas, TX 75244
Phone: (972) 239-4297

#110
Boomers On Bishop
Category: Department Stores
Average Price: Modest
Area: Bishop Arts District, Oak Cliff
Address: 504 N Bishop Ave
Dallas, TX 75208
Phone: (214) 943-1275

#111
Bloomingdale's - Dallas
Category: Outlet Stores
Average Price: Modest
Area: Lake Highlands
Address: 8180 Park Ln
Dallas, TX 75231
Phone: (972) 707-6850

#112
White Rock Soap Gallery
Category: Gift Shops,
Cosmetics & Beauty Supply
Average Price: Modest
Area: Lake Highlands
Address: 10233 E Nw Hwy
Dallas, TX 75238
Phone: (469) 215-5125

#113
Interabang Books
Category: Bookstores
Average Price: Modest
Area: North Dallas
Address: 10720 Preston Rd
Dallas, TX 75230
Phone: (214) 484-4289

#114
Voodoo Chile
Category: Thrift Stores
Average Price: Modest
Area: Lower Greenville
Address: 5643 Bell Ave
Dallas, TX 75206
Phone: (214) 752-0266

#115
Rye 51
Category: Men's Clothing,
Accessories, Shoe Stores
Average Price: Expensive
Area: Uptown
Address: 3699 Mckinney Ave
Dallas, TX 75204
Phone: (214) 780-0202

#116
L Bartlett
Category: Women's Clothing, Shoe Stores
Average Price: Expensive
Area: Uptown
Address: 3699 Mckinney Ave
Dallas, TX 75204
Phone: (214) 521-3500

#117
Dwell On Davis
Category: Women's Clothing
Average Price: Modest
Area: Bishop Arts District, Oak Cliff
Address: 336 W Davis St
Dallas, TX 75208
Phone: (469) 729-9895

#118
Ross Dress For Less
Category: Women's Clothing
Average Price: Inexpensive
Area: East Dallas
Address: 2405 N Haskell Ave
Dallas, TX 75204
Phone: (214) 841-0100

#119
Shoe Mart
Category: Shoe Stores
Average Price: Modest
Area: Farmer's Branch
Address: 11818 Harry Hines Blvd
Dallas, TX 75234
Phone: (972) 243-1348

#120
Upscale For Less
Category: Women's Clothing, Accessories
Average Price: Modest
Area: Farmer's Branch
Address: 11834 Harry Hines Blvd
Dallas, TX 75234
Phone: (972) 481-7886

#121
Aftershock London
Category: Women's Clothing
Average Price: Modest
Area: North Dallas
Address: 13350 Dallas Pkwy
Dallas, TX 75240
Phone: (214) 363-4699

#122
Buffalo Exchange
Category: Men's Clothing, Women's Clothing,
Used, Vintage & Consignment
Average Price: Modest
Area: Lower Greenville
Address: 3424 Greenville Ave
Dallas, TX 75206
Phone: (214) 826-7544

#123
Gypsy House
Category: Thrift Stores, Women's Clothing
Average Price: Modest
Area: Oak Cliff
Address: 421 N Tyler St
Dallas, TX 75208
Phone: (214) 437-3321

#124
Whole Earth Provision
Category: Shoe Stores,
Outdoor Gear, Toy Stores
Average Price: Modest
Area: Lower Greenville
Address: 5400 E Mockingbird Ln
Dallas, TX 75206
Phone: (214) 824-7444

#125
Centre
Category: Women's Clothing,
Men's Clothing, Shoe Stores
Average Price: Modest
Area: Upper Greenville
Address: 5307 E Mockingbird Ln
Dallas, TX 75206
Phone: (214) 821-2028

#126
Furniture Buy Consignment
Category: Furniture Stores, Home Decor
Average Price: Modest
Area: North Dallas
Address: 11722 Marsh Ln
Dallas, TX 75229
Phone: (214) 358-0437

#127
Birchwood
Category: Art Galleries, Home
Decor, Furniture Stores
Average Price: Modest
Area: Lower Greenville
Address: 2726 N Henderson Ave
Dallas, TX 75206
Phone: (214) 774-9181

#128
Keeks Designer Handbags
Category: Vintage & Consignment
Average Price: Expensive
Area: North Dallas
Address: 18208 Preston Dr
Dallas, TX 75252
Phone: (214) 797-8524

#129
DSW Designer Shoe Warehouse
Category: Shoe Stores, Accessories
Average Price: Expensive
Area: Lake Highlands
Address: 8160 Park Ln
Dallas, TX 75231
Phone: (214) 971-7085

#130
Gomez Western Wear
Category: Fashion
Average Price: Modest
Area: North Dallas
Address: 11253 Harry Hines Blvd
Dallas, TX 75229
Phone: (972) 488-3999

#131
**J.Crew Mercantile - The
Shops At Park Lane**
Category: Men's Clothing, Women's Clothing
Average Price: Modest
Area: Lake Highlands
Address: 8020 Park Ln
Dallas, TX 75231
Phone: (469) 232-4563

#132
Nordstrom
Category: Department Stores, Men's
Clothing, Women's Clothing
Average Price: Expensive
Area: North Dallas
Address: 8687 N Central Expy
Dallas, TX 75225
Phone: (214) 231-3900

#133
Urban Outfitters
Category: Men's Clothing, Women's
Clothing, Home Decor
Average Price: Modest
Area: Upper Greenville
Address: 5331 E Mockingbird Ln
Dallas, TX 75206
Phone: (214) 821-4371

#134
Rockwell Antiques
Category: Antiques
Average Price: Modest
Area: Design District
Address: 1500 Market Center Blvd
Dallas, TX 75207
Phone: (877) 705-8570

#135
Dude, Sweet Chocolate
Category: Chocolatiers &
Shops, Desserts, Gift Shops
Average Price: Modest
Area: Bishop Arts District, Oak Cliff
Address: 408 W 8th St
Dallas, TX 75208
Phone: (214) 943-5943

#136
Hollywood Five & Dime
Category: Men's Clothing, Shoe Stores
Average Price: Modest
Area: Exposition Park, Fair Park
Address: 3621 Parry Ave
Dallas, TX 75226
Phone: (214) 827-1680

#137
Whole Earth Provision Co.
Category: Shoe Stores
Average Price: Modest
Area: North Dallas
Address: 11700 Preston Rd
Dallas, TX 75230
Phone: (972) 861-5700

#138
MYBAG Handbags
Category: Accessories, Leather Goods
Average Price: Modest
Area: East Dallas
Address: 709 N Haskell Ave
Dallas, TX 75246
Phone: (214) 634-4900

#139
ES Collection
Category: Men's Clothing, Swimwear
Average Price: Expensive
Area: Oak Lawn
Address: 3926 Cedar Springs Rd
Dallas, TX 75219
Phone: (214) 599-8830

#140
Skivvies
Category: Men's Clothing,
Swimwear, Outlet Stores
Average Price: Modest
Area: Oak Lawn
Address: 4001-C Cedar Springs Rd
Dallas, TX 75219
Phone: (214) 559-4955

#141
Francesca's Collections
Category: Jewelry, Women's
Clothing, Accessories
Average Price: Modest
Area: North Dallas
Address: 10720 Preston Rd
Dallas, TX 75230
Phone: (214) 891-9866

#142
Dolly Python
Category: Vintage &Consignment
Average Price: Modest
Area: East Dallas
Address: 1916 N Haskell Ave
Dallas, TX 75204
Phone: (214) 887-3434

#143
Bishop Ranch
Category: Home Decor
Average Price: Modest
Area: Bishop Arts District, Oak Cliff
Address: 332 W Davis St
Dallas, TX 75208
Phone: (469) 930-8963

#144
Gratitude
Category: Used, Vintage & Consignment
Average Price: Modest
Area: Oak Lawn
Address: 3613 Fairmount St
Dallas, TX 75219
Phone: (214) 522-2921

#145
Sid Mashburn
Category: Men's Clothing, Accessories
Average Price: Expensive
Area: Uptown
Address: 3319 Knox St
Dallas, TX 75205
Phone: (214) 443-6101

#146
Kittsona
Category: Home Decor, Women's
Clothing, Accessories
Average Price: Modest
Area: North Dallas
Address: 6025 Royal Ln
Dallas, TX 75230
Phone: (972) 730-3997

#147
Turquoise And Lavender
Category: Perfume, Jewelry, Home Decor
Average Price: Modest
Area: Lakewood
Address: 1924 Abrams Rd
Dallas, TX 75214
Phone: (214) 502-1162

#148
Heart In Hand Gallery
Category: Tattoo, Piercing, Accessories
Average Price: Modest
Area: Deep Ellum
Address: 2614 Elm St
Dallas, TX 75226
Phone: (469) 776-5667

#149
Loft
Category: Accessories, Women's Clothing
Average Price: Modest
Area: North Dallas
Address: 8687 N Central Expy
Dallas, TX 75225
Phone: (214) 363-3205

#150
Simi Sue
Category: Women's Clothing
Average Price: Modest
Area: North Dallas
Address: 11536 Harry Hines Blvd
Dallas, TX 75229
Phone: (972) 247-2526

#151
LA REUNION Jewelry
Category: Accessories, Jewelry
Average Price: Modest
Area: Deep Ellum
Address: 2602B Main St
Dallas, TX 75226
Phone: (469) 579-9339

#152
Cost Plus World Market
Category: Furniture Stores, Home Decor
Average Price: Modest
Area: North Dallas
Address: 13912 Dallas Pkwy
Dallas, TX 75240
Phone: (972) 367-0090

#153
Harry Hines Bazaar
Category: Flea Markets
Average Price: Modest
Area: North Dallas
Address: 10788 Harry Hines Blvd
Dallas, TX 75220
Phone: (214) 352-2233

#154
LOST Again Antiques & Decor
Category: Antiques, Home
Decor, Furniture Stores
Average Price: Expensive
Area: Design District
Address: 148 Riveredge
Dallas, TX 75207
Phone: (214) 741-4411

#155
Empressive Geodesigns
Category: Home Decor, Art Galleries
Average Price: Modest
Area: Design District
Address: 1339 E Levee St
Dallas, TX 75207
Phone: (214) 343-0000

#156
Antiques Moderne
Category: Antiques, Furniture Reupholstery
Average Price: Modest
Area: Design District
Address: 1208 N Riverfront Blvd
Dallas, TX 75207
Phone: (214) 215-9600

#157
Labels Designer
Consignment Boutique
Category: Women's Clothing
Average Price: Expensive
Area: North Dallas
Address: 18208 Preston Rd
Dallas, TX 75252
Phone: (972) 867-3366

#158
Hillcrest Village
Category: Shopping Centers
Average Price: Inexpensive
Area: North Dallas
Address: 6959 Arapaho Rd
Dallas, TX 75248
Phone: (972) 361-0800

#159
Melissa Benge Collection
Category: Jewelry, Women's Clothing
Average Price: Modest
Area: Lower Greenville
Address: 2823 Henderson St
Dallas, TX 75206
Phone: (214) 821-1777

#160
Ross Dress For Less
Category: Department Stores
Average Price: Inexpensive
Area: Oak Cliff
Address: 655 Wynnewood
Village Shopping Ctr
Dallas, TX 75224
Phone: (214) 943-8208

#161
Nordstrom
Category: Women's Clothing
Average Price: Expensive
Area: North Dallas
Address: 5220 Alpha Rd
Dallas, TX 75240
Phone: (972) 702-0055

#162
Forever 21
Category: Children's Clothing,
Women's Clothing, Accessories
Average Price: Modest
Area: Lake Highlands
Address: 8166 Park Ln
Dallas, TX 75231
Phone: (469) 232-2307

#163
Ann's Health Food Center & Market
Category: Health Markets, Juice
Bars & Smoothies, Grocery
Average Price: Modest
Area: Oak Cliff
Address: 2634 S Zang Blvd
Dallas, TX 75224
Phone: (214) 942-9483

#164
Rethreads
Category: Men's Clothing, Women's Clothing
Average Price: Modest
Area: North Dallas
Address: 12835 Preston Rd
Dallas, TX 75230
Phone: (972) 233-1684

#165
Target
Category: Department Stores
Average Price: Modest
Area: North Dallas
Address: 9440 Marsh Ln
Dallas, TX 75220
Phone: (214) 357-3980

#166
STAG Provisions For Men
Category: Men's Clothing,
Accessories, Shoe Stores
Average Price: Expensive
Area: Uptown
Address: 4525 Cole Ave
Dallas, TX 75205
Phone: (214) 599-2143

#167
The Cozy Cottage
Children's Boutique
Category: Children's Clothing, Toy Stores
Average Price: Modest
Area: Oak Cliff
Address: 1314 W Davis St
Dallas, TX 75208
Phone: (214) 941-1110

#168
Antiques On Bishop
Category: Antiques
Average Price: Modest
Area: Bishop Arts District, Oak Cliff
Address: 336 W 8th St
Dallas, TX 75208
Phone: (214) 680-4960

#169
Carolina Herrera
Category: Accessories, Men's Clothing,
Women's Clothing
Average Price: Modest
Area: North Dallas
Address: 8687 N Central Expy
Dallas, TX 75225
Phone: (469) 232-9002

#170
East & Orient Company
Category: Antiques
Average Price: Modest
Area: Design District
Address: 179 Parkhouse St
Dallas, TX 75207
Phone: (214) 741-1191

#171
Cowboy Cool
Category: Men's Clothing, Women's Clothing
Average Price: Expensive
Area: Uptown
Address: 3699 Mckinney Ave
Dallas, TX 75204
Phone: (214) 521-4500

#172
The Fancy Flea Antique Mall
Category: Antiques
Average Price: Modest
Area: Oak Lawn
Address: 4310 Maple Ave
Dallas, TX 75219
Phone: (214) 261-1005

#173
Sebastian's Closet
Category: Men's Clothing, Bespoke Clothing
Average Price: Expensive
Area: Addison
Address: 5100 Belt Line Rd
Dallas, TX 75254
Phone: (972) 387-0888

#174
Loft
Category: Women's Clothing,
Accessories, Shoe Stores
Average Price: Modest
Area: Uptown
Address: 3699 Mckinney Ave
Dallas, TX 75204
Phone: (469) 547-5766

#175
North Dallas Antique Mall
Category: Antiques
Average Price: Modest
Area: North Dallas
Address: 11722 Marsh Ln
Dallas, TX 75229
Phone: (214) 366-2100

#176
The Little Things
Category: Children's Clothing, Toy Stores
Average Price: Modest
Area: Lower Greenville
Address: 5207 Bonita Ave
Dallas, TX 75206
Phone: (214) 821-3015

#177
Bonobos
Category: Men's Clothing, Personal
Shopping, Formal Wear
Average Price: Exclusive
Area: Lower Greenville
Address: 1901 N Henderson Ave
Dallas, TX 75206
Phone: (469) 334-0661

#178
Designer Silk Gallery
Category: Florists, Home
Decor, Floral Designers
Average Price: Modest
Area: North Dallas
Address: 11311 Harry Hines Blvd
Dallas, TX 75229
Phone: (972) 241-9988

#179
Pink Lucy
Category: Women's Clothing
Average Price: Modest
Area: East Dallas
Address: 4032 Swiss Ave
Dallas, TX 75204
Phone: (214) 613-6117

#180
Tuesday Morning
Category: Department Stores, Home Decor
Average Price: Modest
Area: Lake Highlands
Address: 9384 N Central Expy
Dallas, TX 75231
Phone: (214) 891-9434

#181
Kohl's
Category: Department Stores, Men's Clothing, Women's Clothing
Average Price: Modest
Area: Lakewood
Address: 5750 Skillman St
Dallas, TX 75206
Phone: (214) 368-1204

#182
Jcpenney
Category: Men's Clothing, Women's Clothing
Average Price: Modest
Area: Lake Highlands
Address: 6051 Skillman St
Dallas, TX 75231
Phone: (972) 892-2050

#183
Rose Garden Remake
Category: Used, Vintage & Consignment, Home Decor
Average Price: Modest
Area: Oak Cliff
Address: 835 W Davis St
Dallas, TX 75208
Phone: (214) 941-1333

#184
Canal Clothing
Category: Women's Clothing, Accessories
Average Price: Modest
Area: Lakewood
Address: 6465 E Mockingbird
Dallas, TX 75214
Phone: (214) 343-6177

#185
City View Antique Mall
Category: Antiques, Furniture Stores
Average Price: Modest
Area: Lake Highlands
Address: 6830 Walling Ln
Dallas, TX 75231
Phone: (469) 608-2556

#186
Mine Gifts & Monogram
Category: Embroidery & Crochet
Average Price: Inexpensive
Area: North Dallas
Address: 11536 Harry Hines Blvd
Dallas, TX 75229
Phone: (972) 247-6086

#187
Talbots
Category: Shopping Centers
Average Price: Modest
Area: North Dallas
Address: 13350 Dallas Pkwy
Dallas, TX 75240
Phone: (972) 934-8586

#188
Saks OFF 5TH
Category: Men's Clothing, Women's Clothing
Average Price: Modest
Area: Lake Highlands
Address: 8040 Park Ln
Dallas, TX 75231
Phone: (214) 750-5909

#189
J Crew
Category: Accessories, Men's Clothing, Women's Clothing
Average Price: Expensive
Area: Uptown
Address: 3700 Mckinney Ave
Dallas, TX 75204
Phone: (214) 599-6275

#190
Thrift World Of Dallas
Category: Thrift Stores
Average Price: Inexpensive
Area: North Dallas
Address: 3046 Forest Ln
Dallas, TX 75234
Phone: (972) 481-7800

#191
White House Black Market
Category: Women's Clothing
Average Price: Expensive
Area: North Dallas
Address: 10720 Preston Rd
Dallas, TX 75230
Phone: (214) 987-0110

#192
Disney Store
Category: Gift Shops, Children's Clothing
Average Price: Modest
Area: North Dallas
Address: 8687 North Central Expy
Dallas, TX 75225
Phone: (214) 234-0144

#193
Main Street Mercantile
Category: Used, Vintage & Consignment
Average Price: Modest
Area: Deep Ellum
Address: 2707 Main St
Dallas, TX 75226
Phone: (214) 741-4107

#194
Lorna Jane
Category: Women's Clothing, Sports Wear
Average Price: Expensive
Area: Uptown
Address: 3700 Mckinney Avenue
Dallas, TX 75204
Phone: (469) 930-8408

#195
Kohl's
Category: Department Stores, Men's
Clothing, Women's Clothing
Average Price: Modest
Area: North Dallas
Address: 18224 Preston Rd
Dallas, TX 75252
Phone: (972) 964-7447

#196
The Consignment Solution
Category: Home Decor, Used,
Vintage & Consignment
Average Price: Modest
Area: Lakewood
Address: 1931 Skillman St
Dallas, TX 75206
Phone: (214) 827-8022

#197
99 Cents Only Stores
Category: Discount Store, Party Supplies
Average Price: Inexpensive
Area: North Dallas
Address: 13444 Preston Rd
Dallas, TX 75240
Phone: (972) 386-5999

#198
Stein Mart
Category: Women's Clothing,
Department Stores, Accessories
Average Price: Modest
Area: North Dallas
Address: 14902 Preston Rd
Dallas, TX 75254
Phone: (972) 458-8832

#199
Target
Category: Department Stores
Average Price: Modest
Area: North Dallas
Address: 13131 Montfort Dr
Dallas, TX 75240
Phone: (972) 239-8161

#200
Koslow's Furs
Category: Women's Clothing
Average Price: Modest
Area: Lake Highlands
Address: 8188 Park Ln
Dallas, TX 75231
Phone: (214) 361-6400

#201
Intermix
Category: Women's Clothing
Average Price: Expensive
Area: North Dallas
Address: 8687 N Central Expy
Dallas, TX 75225
Phone: (214) 691-3800

#202
Emeralds To Coconuts
Category: Women's Clothing,
Accessories, Jewelry
Average Price: Modest
Area: Lower Greenville
Address: 2730 N Henderson Ave
Dallas, TX 75206
Phone: (214) 823-3620

#203
DFW Mantiques
Category: Antiques
Average Price: Modest
Area: Bishop Arts District, Oak Cliff
Address: 301 W Eighth St
Dallas, TX 75208
Phone: (214) 941-4195

#204
J.Crew
Category: Accessories, Men's Clothing,
Women's Clothing
Average Price: Modest
Area: North Dallas
Address: 8687 North Central Expy
Dallas, TX 75225
Phone: (214) 987-9700

#205
Splendid
Category: Women's Clothing, Children's
Clothing, Men's Clothing
Average Price: Modest
Area: North Dallas
Address: 8687 N Central Expy
Dallas, TX 75225
Phone: (469) 232-4509

#206
Urban Outfitters
Category: Women's Clothing,
Men's Clothing, Home Decor
Average Price: Modest
Area: North Dallas
Address: 8687 N Central Expy
Dallas, TX 75225
Phone: (214) 361-2001

#207
Jack Retro
Category: Used, Vintage & Consignment
Average Price: Modest
Area: Lower Greenville
Address: 2802 Greenville Ave
Dallas, TX 75206
Phone: (214) 821-5225

#208
Creative Stitches & Gifts
Category: Arts & Crafts, Gift Shops
Average Price: Modest
Area: North Dallas
Address: 12817 Preston Rd
Dallas, TX 75230
Phone: (214) 361-2610

#209
Luxe District Collective
Category: Home Decor, Furniture Stores
Average Price: Modest
Area: Downtown
Address: 920 S Harwood St
Dallas, TX 75201
Phone: (855) 376-9186

#210
Swatch Store
Category: Watches, Accessories
Average Price: Modest
Area: North Dallas
Address: 8687 North Central Expressway
Dallas, TX 75225
Phone: (214) 361-4088

#211
Ann Mashburn
Category: Women's Clothing, Accessories
Average Price: Expensive
Area: Uptown
Address: 3319 Knox St
Dallas, TX 75205
Phone: (214) 443-6100

#212
Mecox Dallas
Category: Home Decor, Antiques
Average Price: Expensive
Area: Uptown
Address: 4532 Cole Ave
Dallas, TX 75205
Phone: (214) 580-3800

#213
World Market
Category: Beer, Wine & Spirits,
Home Decor, Furniture Stores
Average Price: Modest
Area: Upper Greenville
Address: 5500 Greenville Ave
Dallas, TX 75206
Phone: (214) 378-5370

#214
Family Dollar Stores
Category: Department Stores
Average Price: Modest
Area: South Dallas
Address: 3200 S Lancaster Rd
Dallas, TX 75216
Phone: (214) 371-1476

#215
Paper Source
Category: Cards & Stationery, Gift Shops
Average Price: Modest
Area: Uptown
Address: 4525 Cole Ave
Dallas, TX 75205
Phone: (214) 599-2646

#216
Express
Category: Women's Clothing, Accessories
Average Price: Expensive
Area: North Dallas
Address: 13350 Dallas Pkwy
Dallas, TX 75240
Phone: (972) 233-2986

#217
Charming Charlie - Dallas
Category: Accessories, Jewelry
Average Price: Modest
Area: Lake Highlands
Address: 8190 Park Ln
Dallas, TX 75231
Phone: (214) 361-2801

#218
The Gift Stylist
Category: Chocolatiers & Shops, Gift Shops
Average Price: Inexpensive
Area: North Dallas
Address: 16000 Preston Rd
Dallas, TX 75248
Phone: (214) 566-2244

#219
Life Storage
Category: Self Storage, Truck Rental,
Packing Supplies
Average Price: Modest
Area: Upper Greenville
Address: 5720 Milton St
Dallas, TX 75206
Phone: (866) 838-2192

#220
Buckle
Category: Men's Clothing, Women's Clothing
Average Price: Modest
Area: North Dallas
Address: 8687 N Central Expy
Dallas, TX 75225
Phone: (214) 265-7680

#221
Belk
Category: Shoe Stores, Men's Clothing,
Women's Clothing
Average Price: Modest
Area: North Dallas
Address: 13350 Dallas Pkwy
Dallas, TX 75240
Phone: (972) 702-7100

#222
Nuvo
Category: Home Decor, Jewelry
Average Price: Expensive
Area: Oak Lawn
Address: 3311OAK Lawn Ave
Dallas, TX 75219
Phone: (214) 522-6886

#223
Steven Alan
Category: Women's Clothing,
Men's Clothing, Accessories
Average Price: Expensive
Area: Uptown
Address: 3205 Knox St
Dallas, TX 75205
Phone: (214) 306-4849

#224
Circa20c
Category: Furniture Stores, Furniture
Reupholstery, Used, Vintage & Consignment
Average Price: Modest
Area: Design District
Address: 1216 N Riverfront Blvd
Dallas, TX 75207
Phone: (214) 704-1787

#225
Avenue
Category: Accessories, Women's Clothing
Average Price: Modest
Area: Addison
Address: 5301 Belt Line Rd
Dallas, TX 75254
Phone: (972) 239-7217

#226
Karen Millen
Category: Women's Clothing, Accessories
Average Price: Expensive
Area: North Dallas
Address: 13350 Dallas Pkwy
Dallas, TX 75240
Phone: (972) 386-8300

#227
Tuesday Morning
Category: Department Stores
Average Price: Modest
Area: Addison
Address: 14303 Inwood Rd
Farmers Branch, TX 75244
Phone: (972) 991-1905

#228
LY Food MARKET &GIFTS
Category: Specialty Food, Jewelry, Thai
Average Price: Inexpensive
Area: Oak Cliff
Address: 4440 W Illinois Ave
Dallas, TX 75211
Phone: (214) 330-9616

#229
Talulah & Hess
Category: Jewelry, Accessories
Average Price: Modest
Area: Lakewood
Address: 5810 Live Oak St
Dallas, TX 75214
Phone: (214) 821-1927

#230
Target
Category: Department Stores
Average Price: Modest
Area: Lake Highlands
Address: 6419 Skillman St
Dallas, TX 75231
Phone: (214) 348-0240

#231
Athleta
Category: Women's Clothing, Sports Wear
Average Price: Expensive
Area: North Dallas
Address: 10720 Preston Rd
Dallas, TX 75230
Phone: (512) 873-7563

#232
Om Imports
Category: Jewelry
Average Price: Modest
Area: North Dallas
Address: 11464 Harry Hines Blvd
Dallas, TX 75229
Phone: (972) 243-5666

#233
Lovely Bride
Category: Bridal, Accessories
Average Price: Modest
Area: Uptown
Address: 2500 Routh St
Dallas, TX 75201
Phone: (972) 546-1319

#234
Bronco Western Wear LLC
Category: Shoe Stores
Average Price: Modest
Area: North Dallas
Address: 11500 Harry Hines Blvd
Dallas, TX 75229
Phone: (972) 484-4004

#235
Run On!
Category: Sports Wear, Shoe Stores
Average Price: Modest
Area: North Dallas
Address: 11811 Preston Rd
Dallas, TX 75230
Phone: (214) 416-9978

#236
Cutting Corners
Category: Fabric Stores, Home Decor,
Furniture Stores
Average Price: Modest
Area: North Dallas
Address: 13720 Midway Rd
Dallas, TX 75244
Phone: (972) 233-1741

#237
Express Shop
Category: Gift Shops, Beer, Wine & Spirits
Average Price: Modest
Area: Uptown
Address: 200 Crescent Ct
Dallas, TX 75201
Phone: (214) 855-2060

#238
Bcbgeneration
Category: Women's Clothing
Average Price: Modest
Area: North Dallas
Address: 13350 Dallas Pkwy
Dallas, TX 75240
Phone: (972) 980-9815

#239
Valley View Center
Category: Shopping Centers
Average Price: Inexpensive
Area: North Dallas
Address: 13331 Preston Rd
Dallas, TX 75201
Phone: (972) 661-2939

#240
Trader Joe's
Category: Grocery
Average Price: Modest
Area: North Dallas
Address: 7939 Walnut Hill Ln
Dallas, TX 75230
Phone: (214) 346-6579

#241
2shea Baby
Category: Children's Clothing,
Baby Gear & Furniture
Average Price: Modest
Area: Lakewood
Address: 6224 La Vista Dr
Dallas, TX 75214
Phone: (469) 312-0886

#242
Marshalls
Category: Department Stores
Average Price: Modest
Area: North Dallas
Address: 7609 Campbell Rd
Dallas, TX 75248
Phone: (972) 248-8494

#243
Marmi
Category: Shoe Stores, Accessories
Average Price: Modest
Area: North Dallas
Address: 13350 Dallas Pkwy
Dallas, TX 75240
Phone: (972) 392-1992

#244
Big Daddy's Convenience Store
Category: Convenience Stores
Average Price: Inexpensive
Area: South Dallas
Address: 4121 Colonial Ave
Dallas, TX 75215
Phone: (214) 428-6203

#245
Rewards
Category: Jewelry, Leather
Goods, Accessories
Average Price: Exclusive
Area: North Dallas
Address: 4230 Lyndon B Johnson Fwy
Dallas, TX 75244
Phone: (800) 292-0195

#246
Lucas Street Antiques
Category: Antiques
Average Price: Expensive
Area: Oak Lawn
Address: 2023 Lucas Dr
Dallas, TX 75219
Phone: (214) 559-9806

#247
The Container Store
Category: Home Decor,
Luggage, Kitchen & Bath
Average Price: Modest
Area: North Dallas
Address: 5203 Alpha Rd
Dallas, TX 75240
Phone: (972) 458-9228

#248
Nicole Kwon Concept Store
Category: Women's Clothing
Average Price: Expensive
Area: Uptown
Address: 3699 Mckinney Ave
Dallas, TX 75204
Phone: (214) 526-7000

#249
Photographs Do Not Bend Gallery
Category: Art Galleries,
Antiques, Bookstores
Average Price: Expensive
Area: Design District
Address: 154 Glass St
Dallas, TX 75207
Phone: (214) 969-1852

#250
Callidora Jewelry & Gifts
Category: Jewelry, Gift Shops
Average Price: Modest
Area: Lower Greenville
Address: 2913 Greenville Ave
Dallas, TX 75206
Phone: (214) 515-9188

#251
VOD
Category: Women's Clothing
Average Price: Modest
Area: Victory Park
Address: 2418 Victory Park Ln
Dallas, TX 75219
Phone: (214) 754-0644

#252
A+ Wholesale
Category: Discount Store
Average Price: Modest
Area: North Dallas
Address: 2639 Walnut Hill Ln
Dallas, TX 75229
Phone: (817) 617-1018

#253
H&M
Category: Men's Clothing, Women's Clothing, Children's Clothing
Average Price: Modest
Area: North Dallas
Address: 8687 N Central Expy
Dallas, TX 75225
Phone: (855) 466-7467

#254
Anteks Home Furnishings
Category: Furniture Stores, Home Decor, Rugs
Average Price: Expensive
Area: Design District
Address: 1135 Dragon St
Dallas, TX 75207
Phone: (214) 528-5567

#255
Coldwater Creek
Category: Accessories, Women's Clothing
Average Price: Modest
Area: North Dallas
Address: 8687 N Central Expy
Dallas, TX 75225
Phone: (214) 265-0842

#256
Fino
Category: Men's Clothing
Average Price: Modest
Area: Downtown
Address: 1612 Elm St
Dallas, TX 75201
Phone: (214) 741-7259

#257
Sears Outlet
Category: Outlet Stores, Appliances
Average Price: Expensive
Area: North Dallas
Address: 14060 Dallas Pkwy
Dallas, TX 75240
Phone: (469) 374-0011

#258
Coach
Category: Leather Goods, Accessories
Average Price: Modest
Area: North Dallas
Address: 13350 Dallas Pkwy
Dallas, TX 75240
Phone: (972) 392-1772

#259
Country French Interiors Inc
Category: Antiques
Average Price: Expensive
Area: Design District
Address: 1428 Slocum St
Dallas, TX 75207
Phone: (214) 747-4700

#260
Legacy Antiques
Category: Antiques
Average Price: Modest
Area: Design District
Address: 1406 Slocum St
Dallas, TX 75207
Phone: (214) 748-4606

#261
Goodies From Goodman
Category: Food Delivery Services, Gift Shops
Average Price: Modest
Area: North Dallas
Address: 11390 Grissom Ln
Dallas, TX 75229
Phone: (972) 484-3236

#262
Bottega Veneta
Category: Leather Goods, Accessories
Average Price: Exclusive
Area: North Dallas
Address: 8687 N Central Expy
Dallas, TX 75225
Phone: (214) 265-0136

#263
Metrocrest Resale
Category: Thrift Stores, Accessories, Vintage & Consignment
Average Price: Inexpensive
Area: Carrollton
Address: 2661 Midway Rd
Carrollton, TX 75006
Phone: (972) 250-1900

#264
Wild Wild West
Category: Women's Clothing, Accessories, Souvenir Shops
Average Price: Exclusive
Area: West End, Downtown
Address: 509 Elm St
Dallas, TX 75202
Phone: (214) 655-2880

#265
Sperry
Category: Shoe Stores, Men's
Clothing, Women's Clothing
Average Price: Modest
Area: North Dallas
Address: 8687 N Central Expy
Dallas, TX 75225
Phone: (214) 987-3676

#266
Habitat For Humanity Restore
Category: Home Decor, Building Supplies
Average Price: Inexpensive
Area: Lake Highlands
Address: 6500 Skillman St
Dallas, TX 75231
Phone: (214) 678-2385

#267
Ray-Ban At Northpark Center
Category: Eyewear & Opticians, Accessories
Average Price: Modest
Area: North Dallas
Address: 8687 North Central Expy
Dallas, TX 75225
Phone: (214) 365-0808

#268
John Varvatos
Category: Men's Clothing
Average Price: Modest
Area: North Dallas
Address: 8687 N Central Expy
Dallas, TX 75225
Phone: (469) 480-5480

#269
L'Patricia
Category: Accessories, Women's Clothing
Average Price: Modest
Area: North Dallas
Address: 13331 Preston Rd
Dallas, TX 75240
Phone: (972) 385-1509

#270
The Black Tux
Category: Clothing Rental,
Formal Wear, Men's Clothing
Average Price: Modest
Area: Lower Greenville
Address: 2323 N Henderson Ave
Dallas, TX 75206
Phone: (833) 270-5350

#271
Brookstone Company
Category: Gift Shops, Electronics
Average Price: Modest
Area: North Dallas
Address: 214 Northpark Ctr
Dallas, TX 75225
Phone: (214) 368-0473

#272
Sharon Young Inc-Brockwood
Category: Women's Clothing
Average Price: Modest
Area: Northeast Dallas
Address: 10367 Brockwood Rd
Dallas, TX 75238
Phone: (214) 349-1891

#273
Shu Deals
Category: Shoe Stores
Average Price: Inexpensive
Area: North Dallas
Address: 5812 Lbj Fwy
Dallas, TX 75230
Phone: (214) 710-1227

#274
Accents
Category: Women's Clothing,
Jewelry, Accessories
Average Price: Inexpensive
Area: Upper Greenville
Address: 5331 E Mockingbird Ln
Dallas, TX 75206
Phone: (214) 252-3870

#275
T Art Fashion
Category: Men's Clothing, Wholesale Stores,
Screen Printing/T-Shirt Printing
Average Price: Modest
Area: North Dallas
Address: 11523 Harry Hines Blvd
Dallas, TX 75229
Phone: (972) 488-8016

#276
Target
Category: Department Stores
Average Price: Modest
Area: North Dallas
Address: 16731 Coit Rd
Dallas, TX 75248
Phone: (214) 775-0206

#277
Medallion Shopping Center
Category: Shopping Centers
Average Price: Modest
Area: Lakewood
Address: 6464 Northwest Hwy
Dallas, TX 75214
Phone: (214) 691-6541

#278
J Jill
Category: Accessories, Women's
Clothing, Shoe Stores
Average Price: Modest
Area: North Dallas
Address: 8687 N Central Expy
Dallas, TX 75225
Phone: (469) 232-5401

#279
DSW Designer Shoe Warehouse
Category: Shoe Stores
Average Price: Modest
Area: Addison
Address: 5301 Belt Line Rd
Dallas, TX 75254
Phone: (972) 386-9126

#280
Famous Footwear
Category: Shoe Stores,
Accessories, Sports Wear
Average Price: Modest
Area: Lakewood
Address: 6464 E Nw Hwy Ste 170
Dallas, TX 75214
Phone: (214) 696-5284

#281
Eye Pieces
Category: Eyewear & Opticians,
Optometrists, Accessories
Average Price: Modest
Area: Uptown
Address: 3699 Mckinney Ave
Dallas, TX 75204
Phone: (214) 219-4402

#282
The Toy Maven
Category: Toy Stores
Average Price: Modest
Area: North Dallas
Address: 6025 Royal Ln
Dallas, TX 75230
Phone: (214) 265-9971

#283
Barrington
Category: Luggage, Leather
Goods, Accessories
Average Price: Modest
Area: East Dallas
Address: 2300 N Haskell Ave
Dallas, TX 75204
Phone: (214) 528-6990

#284
Walmart Supercenter
Category: Grocery, Department Stores
Average Price: Inexpensive
Area: North Dallas
Address: 9410 Webb Chapel Rd
Dallas, TX 75220
Phone: (972) 629-0007

#285
Le Louvre French Antiques
Category: Antiques
Average Price: Exclusive
Area: Design District
Address: 1400 Slocum St
Dallas, TX 75207
Phone: (214) 742-2605

#286
Small Pockets
Category: Children's Clothing, Maternity
Wear, Used, Vintage & Consignment
Average Price: Modest
Area: North Dallas
Address: 12300 Inwood Rd
Dallas, TX 75244
Phone: (214) 484-9240

#287
Torrid
Category: Accessories, Women's
Clothing, Plus Size Fashion
Average Price: Modest
Area: Lake Highlands
Address: 8180 Park Ln
Dallas, TX 75231
Phone: (214) 750-3677

#288
Ken's Man's Shop
Category: Men's Clothing
Average Price: Modest
Area: North Dallas
Address: 6025 Royal Ln
Dallas, TX 75230
Phone: (214) 369-5367

#289
Kendra Scott
Category: Jewelry
Average Price: Expensive
Area: Uptown
Address: 3699 Mckinney Ave
Dallas, TX 75204
Phone: (214) 528-4800

#290
Trina Turk Showroom
Category: Fashion
Average Price: Modest
Area: Downtown
Address: 1807 Ross Ave
Dallas, TX 75201
Phone: (214) 999-9450

#291
Apricot Lane Boutique
Category: Women's Clothing
Average Price: Modest
Area: North Dallas
Address: 13350 Dallas Pkwy
Dallas, TX 75240
Phone: (972) 386-6070

#292
Oakley
Category: Eyewear & Opticians,
Accessories, Men's Clothing
Average Price: Expensive
Area: North Dallas
Address: 8687 N Central Expy
Dallas, TX 75225
Phone: (214) 363-7991

#293
Shemara Couture
Category: Men's Clothing,
Women's Clothing, Bridal
Average Price: Modest
Area: Design District
Address: 1300 N Riverfront Blvd
Dallas, TX 75207
Phone: (469) 855-4890

#294
Destination Maternity
Category: Maternity Wear, Accessories,
Women's Clothing
Average Price: Modest
Area: North Dallas
Address: 5539 Lyndon B Johnson Fwy
Dallas, TX 75240
Phone: (972) 788-4115

#295
Lululemon Athletica
Category: Sports Wear,
Women's Clothing, Yoga
Average Price: Expensive
Area: North Dallas
Address: 8687 N Central Expy
Dallas, TX 75225
Phone: (214) 234-0305

#296
Jones Walker
Category: Furniture Stores
Average Price: Expensive
Area: Design District
Address: 1531 Dragon St
Dallas, TX 75206
Phone: (469) 916-5500

#297
Sundance
Category: Women's Clothing,
Accessories, Men's Clothing
Average Price: Expensive
Area: North Dallas
Address: 8687 N Central Expy
Dallas, TX 75225
Phone: (469) 232-2279

#298
Wolford Boutique
Category: Women's Clothing
Average Price: Expensive
Area: North Dallas
Address: 8687 N Central Expy
Dallas, TX 75225
Phone: (214) 265-5515

#299
Zumiez
Category: Men's Clothing, Women's Clothing
Average Price: Modest
Area: North Dallas
Address: 13350 Dallas Pkwy
Dallas, TX 75240
Phone: (972) 851-7296

#300
Pinto Ranch
Category: Shoe Stores, Men's Clothing,
Women's Clothing
Average Price: Expensive
Area: North Dallas
Address: 8687 N Central Expy
Dallas, TX 75225
Phone: (214) 217-6200

#301
Robert Graham
Category: Fashion
Average Price: Expensive
Area: North Dallas
Address: 8687 N Central Expy
Dallas, TX 75225
Phone: (469) 232-9967

#302
Lots Of Furniture
Antiques Warehouse
Category: Antiques, Furniture Stores
Average Price: Expensive
Area: Design District
Address: 910 N Riverfront Blvd
Dallas, TX 75207
Phone: (214) 761-1575

#303
Lane Bryant
Category: Women's Clothing, Shoe Stores
Average Price: Expensive
Area: North Dallas
Address: 16631 Coit Rd
Dallas, TX 75248
Phone: (214) 624-9068

#304
Storybook Blankie
Category: Baby Gear & Furniture, Embroidery
& Crochet, Customized Merchandise
Average Price: Modest
Area: North Dallas
Address: 5930 Royal Ln
Dallas, TX 75230
Phone: (214) 884-8764

#305
Whatchamacallit
Category: Women's Clothing
Average Price: Expensive
Area: Addison
Address: 14999 Preston Rd
Dallas, TX 75254
Phone: (972) 380-1313

#306
Brumley Gardens
Category: Nurseries & Gardening,
Gift Shops, Landscaping
Average Price: Modest
Area: Northeast Dallas
Address: 10540 Church Rd
Dallas, TX 75238
Phone: (214) 343-4900

#307
The Frye Company
Category: Shoe Stores, Accessories
Average Price: Expensive
Area: North Dallas
Address: 8687 N Central Expy
Dallas, TX 75225
Phone: (214) 363-3793

#308
Best Choice
Category: Jewelry, Accessories
Average Price: Inexpensive
Area: North Dallas
Address: 11410 Harry Hines Blvd
Dallas, TX 75229
Phone: (972) 247-4514

#309
The Wild Detectives
Category: Coffee & Tea,
Bars, Bookstores
Average Price: Inexpensive
Area: Bishop Arts District, Oak Cliff
Address: 314 W Eighth St
Dallas, TX 75208
Phone: (214) 942-0108

#310
Tuesday Morning
Category: Department Stores
Average Price: Modest
Area: North Dallas
Address: 12817 Preston Rd
Dallas, TX 75230
Phone: (972) 233-8860

#311
Bodacious Boutique
Category: Accessories, Plus
Size Fashion, Swimwear
Average Price: Expensive
Area: North Dallas
Address: 12835 Preston Rd
Dallas, TX 75230
Phone: (972) 763-0779

#312
Neiman Marcus
Category: Shoe Stores, Men's Clothing,
Women's Clothing
Average Price: Exclusive
Area: North Dallas
Address: 8687 North Central Expy
Dallas, TX 75225
Phone: (214) 363-8311

#313
White House Black Market
Category: Women's Clothing
Average Price: Modest
Area: North Dallas
Address: 8687 N Central Exp'wy
Dallas, TX 75225
Phone: (214) 265-1171

#314
Pier 1 Imports
Category: Department Stores
Average Price: Modest
Area: North Dallas
Address: 10720 Preston Rd
Dallas, TX 75230
Phone: (214) 361-4753

#315
7 For All Mankind
Category: Women's Clothing, Men's Clothing
Average Price: Expensive
Area: North Dallas
Address: 8687 N Central Expy
Dallas, TX 75231
Phone: (214) 346-5914

#316
Build-A-Bear Workshop
Category: Toy Stores, Gift Shops,
Children's Clothing
Average Price: Modest
Area: North Dallas
Address: 13350 Dallas Pkwy
Dallas, TX 75240
Phone: (469) 587-1068

#317
Storage Choice - Farmers Market
Category: Self Storage, Packing Supplies,
Truck Rental
Average Price: Modest
Area: Downtown
Address: 2425 Canton St
Dallas, TX 75226
Phone: (214) 741-1988

#318
Gucci
Category: Men's Clothing, Women's
Clothing, Leather Goods
Average Price: Exclusive
Area: North Dallas
Address: 8687 N Central Expwy
Dallas, TX 75225
Phone: (214) 706-0510

#319
Lou & Grey
Category: Women's Clothing,
Accessories, Jewelry
Average Price: Modest
Area: North Dallas
Address: 8687 N Central Expy
Dallas, TX 75225
Phone: (469) 232-9691

#320
Penguin
Category: Men's Clothing, Women's Clothing
Average Price: Modest
Area: North Dallas
Address: 1030 Northpark Ctr
Dallas, TX 75225
Phone: (214) 750-0952

#321
Lorna Jane
Category: Sports Wear, Women's Clothing
Average Price: Expensive
Area: North Dallas
Address: 8687 N Central Expy
Dallas, TX 75225
Phone: (972) 803-1103

#322
Dallas Embroidery
Category: Embroidery & Crochet,
Screen Printing, Gift Shops
Average Price: Modest
Area: North Dallas
Address: 11536 Harry Hines Blvd
Dallas, TX 75229
Phone: (972) 247-6086

#323
The Vintage House Gift Boutique
Category: Gift Shops
Average Price: Modest
Area: Carrollton
Address: 1101 Beltline Rd
Carrollton, TX 75006
Phone: (972) 242-5616

#324
Beyond The Door
Category: Women's Clothing,
Jewelry, Gift Shops
Average Price: Modest
Area: North Dallas
Address: 2701 Custer Pkwy
Richardson, TX 75080
Phone: (972) 907-9672

#325
Costco Wholesale
Category: Wholesale Stores,
Gas Stations, Pharmacy
Average Price: Modest
Area: North Dallas
Address: 8055 Churchill Way
Dallas, TX 75251
Phone: (469) 680-7546

#326
Jekyll & Hyde Transformation Salon
Category: Vintage & Consignment
Average Price: Modest
Area: Lower Greenville
Address: 2330 N Henderson Ave
Dallas, TX 75206
Phone: (469) 420-0333

#327
Simply Austin Furniture
Category: Furniture Stores
Average Price: Expensive
Area: Bishop Arts District, Oak Cliff
Address: 401 North Bishop Ave
Dallas, TX 75208
Phone: (469) 401-2021

#328
Heritage House Clocks
Category: Clock Repair, Home Decor
Average Price: Modest
Area: Addison
Address: 14450 Midway Rd
Dallas, TX 75244
Phone: (972) 934-3420

#329
Goodwill
Category: Community Service/Non-Profit,
Thrift Stores, Used, Vintage & Consignment
Average Price: Modest
Area: East Dallas
Address: 1919 N Haskell Ave
Dallas, TX 75204
Phone: (214) 823-2481

#330
House Of Angels Catholic Store
Category: Bookstores, Religious Items
Average Price: Inexpensive
Area: North Dallas
Address: 8016 Spring Valley Rd
Dallas, TX 75240
Phone: (214) 245-5311

#331
Catalina 5G
Category: Vintage &
Consignment
Average Price: Modest
Area: Oak Cliff
Address: 1133 S Hampton Rd
Dallas, TX 75208
Phone: (214) 943-6777

#332
Froggie's 5 &10
Category: Toy Stores
Average Price: Modest
Area: Uptown
Address: 3211 Knox St
Dallas, TX 75205
Phone: (214) 522-5867

#333
Suitsupply - Dallas
Category: Men's Clothing, Formal Wear,
Bespoke Clothing
Average Price: Expensive
Area: Uptown
Address: 3700 Mckinney Ave
Dallas, TX 75204
Phone: (214) 306-9856

#334
Banana Republic
Category: Men's Clothing, Women's Clothing
Average Price: Modest
Area: North Dallas
Address: 13335 Noel Rd
Dallas, TX 75240
Phone: (972) 776-4760

#335
Again & Again
Category: Used, Vintage & Consignment
Average Price: Expensive
Area: Design District
Address: 1202 Riverfront Blvd
Dallas, TX 75207
Phone: (214) 746-6300

#336
Ross At Peak
Category: Vintage & Consignment
Average Price: Inexpensive
Area: East Dallas
Address: 4233 Ross Ave
Dallas, TX 75334
Phone: (214) 682-4794

#337
Lululemon Athletica
Category: Sports Wear
Average Price: Expensive
Area: Uptown
Address: 3201 Knox St
Dallas, TX 75205
Phone: (214) 443-0438

#338
Walmart Supercenter
Category: Grocery, Department Stores
Average Price: Expensive
Area: North Dallas
Address: 15757 Coit Rd
Dallas, TX 75248
Phone: (972) 235-0681

#339
ECCO
Category: Shoe Stores
Average Price: Modest
Area: North Dallas
Address: 13350 Dallas Pkwy
Dallas, TX 75240
Phone: (972) 385-2232

#340
Benny Jacks Antiques
Category: Antiques
Average Price: Expensive
Area: East Dallas
Address: 1920 N Haskell Ave
Dallas, TX 75204
Phone: (214) 238-3740

#341
May's Beads
Category: Jewelry, Accessories
Average Price: Modest
Area: North Dallas
Address: 11536 Harry Hines Blvd
Dallas, TX 75229
Phone: (832) 265-2202

#342
Charlotte Russe
Category: Women's Clothing, Accessories
Average Price: Inexpensive
Area: North Dallas
Address: 917 Northpark Ctr
Dallas, TX 75225
Phone: (214) 692-5222

#343
Dallas Comiccon Fanexpo Dallas
Category: Venues & Event
Spaces, Comic Books
Average Price: Modest
Area: Downtown
Address: 650 S Griffin St
Dallas, TX 75202
Phone: (214) 939-2750

#344
World Foot Locker
Category: Shoe Stores
Average Price: Modest
Area: North Dallas
Address: 727 Northpark Ctr
Dallas, TX 75225
Phone: (214) 373-0064

#345
The Finicky Flea
Category: Electronics, Home Decor
Average Price: Modest
Area: Lakewood
Address: 6646 E Lovers Ln
Dallas, TX 75214
Phone: (682) 292-5151

#346
Dallas Tattoo And Arts Company
Category: Art Galleries, Tattoo
Average Price: Modest
Area: East Dallas
Address: 2712 Live Oak St
Dallas, TX 75204
Phone: (469) 334-0469

#347
Singer & Monk
Category: Hats
Average Price: Modest
Area: Bishop Arts District, Oak Cliff
Address: 506 North Bishop Ave
Dallas, TX 75208
Phone: (214) 609-8208

#348
Super Mercado Monterrey
Category: Grocery
Average Price: Modest
Area: Oak Cliff
Address: 300 E Jefferson Blvd
Dallas, TX 75203
Phone: (214) 943-1086

#349
Studio 6 Fitness
Category: Barre Classes,
Pilates, Women's Clothing
Average Price: Modest
Area: North Dallas
Address: 11909 Preston Rd
Dallas, TX 75230
Phone: (972) 239-2626

#350
Chango Botanica
Category: Spiritual Shop
Average Price: Modest
Area: Oak Cliff
Address: 1405 W Davis St
Dallas, TX 75208
Phone: (214) 941-4119

#351
Hollister
Category: Men's Clothing, Women's Clothing
Average Price: Modest
Area: North Dallas
Address: 8687 N Central Expy
Dallas, TX 75225
Phone: (214) 360-7520

#352
Metropark
Category: Fashion
Average Price: Modest
Area: North Dallas
Address: 8687 N Central Expy
Dallas, TX 75225
Phone: (214) 360-9636

#353
Walmart Supercenter
Category: Grocery, Department Stores
Average Price: Inexpensive
Area: North Dallas
Address: 13739 N Central Expy
Dallas, TX 75243
Phone: (972) 656-2501

#354
Ten Of Arts Gifts
Category: Home Decor, Gift Shops, Hats
Average Price: Modest
Area: Carrollton
Address: 1105 S Broadway St
Carrollton, TX 75006
Phone: (972) 242-3357

#355
Barnes & Noble Booksellers
Category: Toy Stores, Bookstores, Gift Shops
Average Price: Modest
Area: Addison
Address: 5301 Belt Line Rd
Dallas, TX 75254
Phone: (972) 980-0853

#356
La Fiesta Fruits & Gifts
Category: Fruits & Veggies, Gift Shops
Average Price: Modest
Area: Downtown
Address: 1627 Pacific Ave
Dallas, TX 75201
Phone: (214) 740-9967

#357
Abercrombie & Fitch
Category: Fashion
Average Price: Modest
Area: North Dallas
Address: 13350 Dallas Pkwy
Dallas, TX 75240
Phone: (972) 233-1832

#358
Ugly Christmas Sweater Shop
Category: Pop-Up Shops
Average Price: Modest
Area: Upper Greenville
Address: 5331 E Mockingbird Ln
Dallas, TX 75206
Phone: (469) 449-4440

#359
Payless Shoesource
Category: Shoe Stores, Accessories
Average Price: Modest
Area: Oak Cliff
Address: 3230 W Davis St
Dallas, TX 75211
Phone: (214) 330-1081

#360
Summer Classics Dallas
Category: Outdoor Furniture Stores,
Home Decor, Furniture Stores
Average Price: Modest
Area: Uptown
Address: 4514 Travis St
Dallas, TX 75205
Phone: (469) 620-6853

#361
Z Gallerie
Category: Furniture Stores,
Home Decor, Gift Shops
Average Price: Expensive
Area: North Dallas
Address: 5225 Alpha Rd
Dallas, TX 75240
Phone: (972) 458-8266

#362
La Mariposa
Category: Women's Clothing, Accessories
Average Price: Modest
Area: North Dallas
Address: 13350 Dallas Pkwy
Dallas, TX 75240
Phone: (972) 239-7173

#363
Thrift Giant
Category: Thrift Stores
Average Price: Inexpensive
Area: North Dallas
Address: 10544 Harry Hines Blvd
Dallas, TX 75220
Phone: (972) 619-7900

#364
Larger Than Life
Category: Vintage &Consignment
Average Price: Modest
Area: North Dallas
Address: 12817 Preston Rd
Dallas, TX 75230
Phone: (214) 342-8550

#365
Pan-African Connection
Category: Art Galleries, Accessories
Average Price: Modest
Area: South Dallas
Address: 4466 S Marsalis Ave
Dallas, TX 75216
Phone: (214) 943-8262

#366
Anonymously Yours
Category: Vintage & Consignment
Average Price: Modest
Area: Northeast Dallas
Address: 9310 Forest Ln
Dallas, TX 75243
Phone: (214) 341-4618

#367
Dallas Antique Company
Category: Antiques
Average Price: Modest
Area: Downtown
Address: 920 S Harwood St
Dallas, TX 75201
Phone: (214) 945-1139

#368
Big Lots - Dallas: Oak Cliff
Category: Furniture Stores, Department
Stores, Home Decor
Average Price: Inexpensive
Area: Oak Cliff
Address: 2128 Fort Worth Ave
Dallas, TX 75211
Phone: (214) 946-1827

#369
Central Market
Category: Grocery
Average Price: Modest
Area: Upper Greenville
Address: 5750 Lovers Ln
Dallas, TX 75206
Phone: (214) 234-7000

#370
Lucky Brand
Category: Men's Clothing
Average Price: Modest
Area: Uptown
Address: 3699 Mckinney Ave
Dallas, TX 75204
Phone: (214) 521-4226

#371
Harry Hines Army Store
Category: Department Stores
Average Price: Modest
Area: North Dallas
Address: 11274 Harry Hines Blvd
Dallas, TX 75229
Phone: (972) 243-6707

#372
Game Over Videogames
Category: Video Game Stores
Average Price: Modest
Area: Addison
Address: 3719 Belt Line Rd
Dallas, TX 75001
Phone: (972) 620-4263

#373
Sweet As Sugar Children's Boutique
Category: Children's Clothing, Accessories
Average Price: Modest
Area: Uptown
Address: 3699 Mckinney Ave
Dallas, TX 75204
Phone: (469) 399-7909

#374
Old Navy
Category: Men's Clothing, Women's Clothing
Average Price: Inexpensive
Area: North Dallas
Address: 13250 Dallas Pkwy
Dallas, TX 75240
Phone: (972) 776-4770

#375
Half Of Half Name Brand Clothing
Category: Shoe Stores, Men's Clothing,
Women's Clothing
Average Price: Modest
Area: North Dallas
Address: 521 W Campbell Rd
Richardson, TX 75080
Phone: (972) 234-9300

#376
Sam's Club
Category: Department Stores
Average Price: Modest
Area: Lake Highlands
Address: 6185 Retail Rd
Dallas, TX 75231
Phone: (214) 382-2297

#377
Family Dollar
Category: Department Stores
Average Price: Modest
Area: Oak Cliff
Address: 113 E Jefferson Blvd
Dallas, TX 75203
Phone: (214) 946-8532

#378
Forestwood Antique Mall
Category: Antiques, JewelryRepair
Average Price: Expensive
Area: North Dallas
Address: 5333 Forest Ln
Dallas, TX 75244
Phone: (972) 661-0001

#379
Fiesta Mart
Category: Grocery
Average Price: Modest
Area: North Dallas
Address: 9727 Webb Chapel Rd
Dallas, TX 75220
Phone: (214) 353-7650

#380
Pier 1 Imports
Category: Kitchen & Bath, Home Decor
Average Price: Modest
Area: Lakewood
Address: 138 Medallion Ctr
Dallas, TX 75214
Phone: (214) 363-4419

#381
Spanx
Category: Women's Clothing
Average Price: Modest
Area: North Dallas
Address: 8687 N Central Expy
Dallas, TX 75225
Phone: (469) 232-9289

#382
A Honey Of A Deal & Company
Category: Accessories,
Women's Clothing, Jewelry
Average Price: Modest
Area: Carrollton
Address: 1106 S Elm St Carrollton, TX 75006
Phone: (972) 446-5654

#383
World Of Goods
Category: Department Stores
Average Price: Inexpensive
Area: Lake Highlands
Address: 10677 E Northwest Hwy
Dallas, TX 75238
Phone: (214) 342-8231

#384
SN Home Linens
Category: Interior Design,
Home Decor
Average Price: Modest
Area: Oak Cliff
Address: 206 W Jefferson Blvd
Dallas, TX 75208
Phone: (214) 946-9927

#385
La Ranchera Supermaket
Category: Grocery
Average Price: Inexpensive
Area: East Dallas
Address: 4823 Bryan St
Dallas, TX 75204
Phone: (214) 821-3414

#386
Coach
Category: Leather Goods,
Accessories
Average Price: Expensive
Area: North Dallas
Address: 8687 N Central Expy
Dallas, TX 75225
Phone: (214) 696-1772

#387
Marco Polo Florist
Category: Florists, Home Decor, Gift Shops
Average Price: Modest
Area: North Dallas
Address: 17390 Preston Rd
Dallas, TX 75252
Phone: (469) 828-7705

#388
Epiphany For Men
Category: Men's Clothing
Average Price: Modest
Area: Bishop Arts District, Oak Cliff
Address: 413 N Bishop Ave
Dallas, TX 75208
Phone: (214) 946-4413

#389
Revolve Modern
Category: Furniture Stores
Average Price: Modest
Area: Design District
Address: 163 Howell St
Dallas, TX 75207
Phone: (469) 867-8360

#390
Knox Street Antiques
Category: Antiques
Average Price: Expensive
Area: Uptown
Address: 3319 Knox St
Dallas, TX 75205
Phone: (214) 521-8888

#391
Q Clothier
Category: Bespoke Clothing, Men's Clothing
Average Price: Expensive
Area: Uptown
Address: 3699 Mckinney Ave
Dallas, TX 75204
Phone: (214) 780-9888

#392
Tory Burch
Category: Accessories, Women's Clothing
Average Price: Expensive
Area: North Dallas
Address: 8687 N Central Expy
Dallas, TX 75225
Phone: (214) 361-2299

#393
Bricks & Minifigs
Category: Toy Stores
Average Price: Modest
Area: North Dallas
Address: 12817 Preston Rd
Dallas, TX 75230
Phone: (469) 906-6042

#394
Inessa Stewarts Antique
Design Center
Category: Antiques
Average Price: Expensive
Area: Design District
Address: 1643 Dragon St
Dallas, TX 75207
Phone: (214) 742-5800

#395
Valentino
Category: Women's Clothing, Men's Clothing
Average Price: Exclusive
Area: North Dallas
Address: N Park Ctr
Dallas, TX 75225
Phone: (214) 750-5707

#396
Ralph Austin Jewelers
Category: Jewelry
Average Price: Modest
Area: Lakewood
Address: 1905 Skillman St
Dallas, TX 75206
Phone: (214) 827-3371

#397
River Regency - Antiques & Modern
Category: Antiques, Furniture Stores
Average Price: Expensive
Area: Design District
Address: 1500 N Riverfront Blvd
Dallas, TX 75207
Phone: (214) 760-8779

#398
Gariani Menswear
Category: Men's Clothing, Formal Wear,
Bespoke Clothing
Average Price: Modest
Area: Addison
Address: 15340 Dallas Pkwy
Dallas, TX 75248
Phone: (972) 661-0104

#399
Walmart Supercenter
Category: Grocery, Department Stores
Average Price: Inexpensive
Area: Northeast Dallas
Address: 9301 Forest Ln
Dallas, TX 75243
Phone: (972) 437-9146

#400
Lauren Belle Jewelry
Category: Jewelry
Average Price: Modest
Area: Uptown
Address: 4514 Cole Ave
Dallas, TX 75205
Phone: (214) 559-7113

#401
Amigo's Pottery
Category: Home Decor
Average Price: Modest
Area: Downtown
Address: 1915 Cadiz St
Dallas, TX 75201
Phone: (214) 752-2281

#402
AG Jeans
Category: Women's Clothing, Men's Clothing
Average Price: Modest
Area: North Dallas
Address: 8687 N Central Expy
Dallas, TX 75225
Phone: (972) 993-1582

#403
Beads Of Splendor
Category: Jewelry, Accessories, Art Classes
Average Price: Modest
Area: Lakewood
Address: 9047 Garland Rd
Dallas, TX 75218
Phone: (214) 824-2777

#404
Deep Ellum Art Co
Category: Music Venues, Venues & Event
Spaces, Art Galleries
Average Price: Inexpensive
Area: Deep Ellum
Address: 3200 Commerce St
Dallas, TX 75226
Phone: (214) 697-8086

#405
Designer Furniture 4 Less
Category: Furniture Stores,
Mattresses, Home Decor
Average Price: Modest
Area: Farmer's Branch
Address: 14009 N Stemmons Fwy
Dallas, TX 75234
Phone: (972) 488-4040

#406
Fossil Store
Category: Accessories, Watches
Average Price: Modest
Area: North Dallas
Address: 8687 N. Central
Dallas, TX 75225
Phone: (214) 361-5338

#407
Dirt Cheap
Category: Discount Store
Average Price: Modest
Area: Carrollton
Address: 3407 Trinity Mills Rd.
Dallas, TX 75287
Phone: (972) 307-2343

#408
Nike Brand
Category: Shoe Stores, Sports Wear
Average Price: Expensive
Area: North Dallas
Address: 8687 N Central Expwy
Dallas, TX 75225
Phone: (214) 363-4127

#409
Guess
Category: Accessories, Women's Clothing
Average Price: Modest
Area: North Dallas
Address: 8687 N Central Expy
Dallas, TX 75225
Phone: (214) 739-8195

#410
Muzeion
Category: Art Galleries, Jewelry
Average Price: Expensive
Area: Design District
Address: 1113 Dragon St
Dallas, TX 75207
Phone: (214) 998-4803

#411
Twosha Beauty Bar
Category: Hair Extensions, Accessories
Average Price: Expensive
Area: North Dallas
Address: 8553 Westchester Dr.
Dallas, TX 75225
Phone: (214) 284-0422

#412
Charming Florals & Finds
Category: Florists, Gift Shops,
Wedding Planning
Average Price: Modest
Area: Downtown
Address: 901 Main St
Dallas, TX 75202
Phone: (972) 308-6060

#413
Herve Leger
Category: Women's Clothing, Accessories
Average Price: Modest
Area: North Dallas
Address: 8687 N Central Expy
Dallas, TX 75231
Phone: (214) 987-3420

#414
Life Storage
Category: Self Storage, Packing Supplies
Average Price: Modest
Area: Oak Lawn
Address: 4640 Harry Hines Blvd
Dallas, TX 75235
Phone: (866) 838-2192

#415
Riddell Rare Maps & Fine Prints
Category: Antiques, Art Galleries
Average Price: Modest
Area: Oak Lawn
Address: 3104 Fairmount St
Dallas, TX 75201
Phone: (214) 953-0601

#416
Stuart Weitzman
Category: Fashion
Average Price: Modest
Area: North Dallas
Address: 8687 N Central Expy
Dallas, TX 75225
Phone: (214) 369-0022

#417
Blue Print Store
Category: Antiques, Furniture Stores
Average Price: Exclusive
Area: Uptown
Address: 2707 Fairmount
Dallas, TX 75201
Phone: (214) 954-9511

#418
**Red Wing Shoes By
Kevin's Work Boots**
Category: Shoe Stores
Average Price: Expensive
Area: North Dallas
Address: 10016 Monroe Dr
Dallas, TX 75229
Phone: (214) 353-9402

#419
Family Dollar
Category: Discount Store
Average Price: Modest
Area: Oak Cliff
Address: 3230 Falls Dr
Dallas, TX 75211
Phone: (214) 337-6606

#420
Prisoseni
Category: Men's Clothing, Bespoke Clothing
Average Price: Expensive
Area: Northeast Dallas, North Dallas
Address: 10000 N Central Expy
Dallas, TX 75231
Phone: (214) 733-1029

#421
Sam Moon Luggage & Gifts
Category: Jewelry, Luggage, Watches
Average Price: Inexpensive
Area: North Dallas
Address: 11637 Harry Hines Blvd
Dallas, TX 75229
Phone: (972) 484-3084

#422
PB&J Thrift And Consignment
Category: Thrift Stores, Used,
Vintage & Consignment
Average Price: Modest
Area: Oak Cliff
Address: 912 W Jefferson
Dallas, TX 75208
Phone: (214) 942-1377

#423
Everything But Water
Category: Women's Clothing, Swimwear
Average Price: Expensive
Area: North Dallas
Address: 8687 N Central Expy
Dallas, TX 75225
Phone: (214) 987-2884

#424
Bijou Luxury Consignment
Category: Women's Clothing, Accessories
Average Price: Expensive
Area: Design District
Address: 1430 Dragon St
Dallas, TX 75207
Phone: (214) 760-1610

#425
Dressmyway
Category: Women's Clothing, Bridal
Average Price: Modest
Area: Design District
Address: 1300 N Riverfront Blvd
Dallas, TX 75207
Phone: (888) 339-3135

#426
Daiso Japan
Category: Discount Store
Average Price: Inexpensive
Area: Carrollton
Address: 2540 Old Denton
Rd Carrollton, TX 75006
Phone: (972) 242-4675

#427
Spinster Records
Category: Vinyl Records
Average Price: Modest
Area: Oak Cliff
Address: 829 W Davis St
Dallas, TX 75208
Phone: (972) 598-0814

#428
Accessory Concierge
Category: Accessories
Average Price: Modest
Area: Lake Highlands
Address: 9603 White Rock Trl
Dallas, TX 75238
Phone: (817) 575-7020

#429
Terry Costa
Category: Bridal, Accessories, Formal Wear
Average Price: Modest
Area: North Dallas
Address: 12817 Preston Rd
Dallas, TX 75230
Phone: (972) 385-6100

#430
Autry's Grocery Store
Category: Grocery
Average Price: Inexpensive
Area: South Dallas
Address: 4903 S Lancaster Rd
Dallas, TX 75216
Phone: (214) 375-6998

#431
Fossil Store
Category: Watches, Accessories,
Leather Goods
Average Price: Expensive
Area: North Dallas
Address: 13350 N Dallas Pkwy
Dallas, TX 75240
Phone: (972) 386-4212

#432
Tommy Bahama
Category: Men's Clothing, Women's Clothing
Average Price: Modest
Area: North Dallas
Address: 13350 Dallas Pkwy
Dallas, TX 75240
Phone: (214) 540-8628

#433
BCBGMAXAZRIA
Category: Women's Clothing, Shoe Stores
Average Price: Expensive
Area: North Dallas
Address: 13350 Dallas Pkwy
Dallas, TX 75240
Phone: (972) 726-0277

#434
Banana Republic
Category: Men's Clothing,
Women's Clothing, Jewelry
Average Price: Modest
Area: Uptown
Address: 3699 Mckinney Ave
Dallas, TX 75204
Phone: (214) 559-0182

#435
Hobbytown USA - Dallas
Category: Toy Stores, Hobby Shops
Average Price: Modest
Area: Lakewood
Address: 6060 E Mockingbird Ln
Dallas, TX 75206
Phone: (214) 987-4744

#436
Tuesday Morning
Category: Kitchen & Bath, Home Decor
Average Price: Inexpensive
Area: Lakewood
Address: 6465 Mockingbird Ln
Dallas, TX 75214
Phone: (214) 828-9303

#437
Blooms Candy & Soda Pop Shop
Category: Candy Stores, Gift Shops
Average Price: Modest
Area: Carrollton
Address: 1106 W Main St
Carrollton, TX 75006
Phone: (972) 416-5230

#438
Lower Greenville Jewelry Workshop
Category: Jewelry, Watch Repair,
Jewelry Repair
Average Price: Inexpensive
Area: Lower Greenville
Address: 2917 Greenville Ave
Dallas, TX 75206
Phone: (214) 826-4454

#439
Dots
Category: Accessories, Women's Clothing
Average Price: Modest
Area: Oak Cliff
Address: 241 Wynnewood Village Shp Ctr
Dallas, TX 75224
Phone: (214) 948-4889

#440
The North Face
Category: Outdoor Gear,
Sports Wear, Shoe Stores
Average Price: Expensive
Area: North Dallas
Address: 8687 N Central Expy
Dallas, TX 75225
Phone: (214) 987-1436

#441
Dallas Silversmiths
Category: Jewelry, Gold Buyers,
Refinishing Services
Average Price: Modest
Area: North Dallas
Address: 11126 Shady Trl
Dallas, TX 75229
Phone: (972) 620-8866

#442
Thrift Shop
Category: Thrift Stores
Average Price: Inexpensive
Area: Lake Highlands
Address: 11411 E Northwest Hwy
Dallas, TX 75218
Phone: (214) 340-2000

#443
89 Cents & Up Jewelry
Category: Jewelry
Average Price: Modest
Area: North Dallas
Address: 11500 Harry Hines Blvd
Dallas, TX 75229
Phone: (972) 243-6733

#444
Citysquare Thrift Store
Category: Thrift Stores
Average Price: Inexpensive
Area: East Dallas
Address: 1213 N Washington
Dallas, TX 75204
Phone: (214) 887-8800

#445
Al's Formal Wear
Category: Men's Clothing
Average Price: Expensive
Area: Oak Lawn
Address: 3400 Oak Lawn Ave
Dallas, TX 75219
Phone: (214) 520-8897

#446
Jen Mauldin Gallery
Category: Art Galleries
Average Price: Modest
Area: Bishop Arts District, Oak Cliff
Address: 408 N Bishop Ave
Dallas, TX 75208
Phone: (214) 954-7629

#447
Wilene Creations
Category: Women's Clothing
Average Price: Expensive
Area: Oak Cliff
Address: 215 W Jefferson Blvd
Dallas, TX 75208
Phone: (214) 946-2880

#448
**Sample House
And Candle Shop**
Category: Candle Stores
Average Price: Modest
Area: North Dallas
Address: 10720 Preston Rd
Dallas, TX 75230
Phone: (214) 365-8085

#449
Roma Boots
Category: Shoe Stores
Average Price: Modest
Area: Lake Highlands
Address: 8060 Park Ln
Dallas, TX 75231
Phone: (888) 612-6264

#450
Cache'women's Apparel
Category: Women's Clothing
Average Price: Modest
Area: North Dallas
Address: 13350 Dallas Pkwy
Dallas, TX 75240
Phone: (972) 458-8505

#451
Lululemon Athletica
Category: Sports Wear, Women's Clothing
Average Price: Expensive
Area: North Dallas
Address: 13350 N Dallas Pkwy
Dallas, TX 75240
Phone: (972) 385-2316

#452
Amanda Sterett Design
Category: Jewelry
Average Price: Modest
Area: Oak Lawn
Address: 3515 Cedar Springs Rd
Dallas, TX 75219
Phone: (214) 774-4783

#453
Uno De 50
Category: Fashion, Jewelry
Average Price: Expensive
Area: North Dallas
Address: 13350 Dallas Pkwy
Dallas, TX 75240
Phone: (972) 701-0143

#454
Rally House Alpha
Category: Sports Wear, Gift Shops
Average Price: Modest
Area: North Dallas
Address: 13710 Dallas Pkwy
Dallas, TX 75240
Phone: (972) 661-9491

#455
Jazame Shoes And Accessories
Category: Shoe Stores
Average Price: Modest
Area: North Dallas
Address: 11029 Harry Hines Blvd
Dallas, TX 75229
Phone: (214) 217-0396

#456
Sooz Boutique
Category: Women's Clothing,
Accessories, Shoe Stores
Average Price: Modest
Area: Carrollton
Address: 1100 W Main St
Carrollton, TX 75006
Phone: (972) 446-2410

#457
Diamond & Gold Warehouse
Category: Jewelry, Gold Buyers
Average Price: Modest
Area: North Dallas
Address: 5757 Alpha Rd
Dallas, TX 75240
Phone: (972) 404-4499

#458
Red Pegasus Comics
Category: Comic Books, Bookstores
Average Price: Modest
Area: Oak Cliff
Address: 319 N Bishop Ave
Dallas, TX 75208
Phone: (972) 413-8716

#459
American Eagle Outfitters
Category: Men's Clothing, Women's Clothing
Average Price: Modest
Area: North Dallas
Address: 13350 Dallas Pkwy
Dallas, TX 75240
Phone: (972) 386-7764

#460
Shaman Modifications
Body Piercing Studio
Category: Piercing, Tattoo, Jewelry
Average Price: Expensive
Area: East Dallas
Address: 502 S Fitzhugh Ave
Dallas, TX 75223
Phone: (214) 235-9473

#461
Dallas Gold & Silver Exchange
Category: Watches, Gold Buyers, Jewelry
Average Price: Modest
Area: North Dallas
Address: 13022 Preston Rd
Dallas, TX 75240
Phone: (972) 484-3662

#462
Footaction
Category: Shoe Stores
Average Price: Modest
Area: Oak Cliff
Address: 1070 Wynnewood Village
Shp Ctr Dallas, TX 75224
Phone: (214) 946-7788

#463
Ramirez Boot Shop
Category: Shoe Stores
Average Price: Inexpensive
Area: Oak Cliff
Address: 916 S Llewellyn
Dallas, TX 75208
Phone: (214) 694-0485

#464
Free People
Category: Women's Clothing
Average Price: Expensive
Area: North Dallas
Address: 8687 N Central Expy
Dallas, TX 75225
Phone: (469) 232-9840

#465
Famous Footwear
Category: Accessories,
Shoe Stores, Sports Wear
Average Price: Modest
Area: East Dallas
Address: 2415 N Haskell Ave
Dallas, TX 75204
Phone: (214) 821-3722

#466
Boot Barn
Category: Men's Clothing, Women's Clothing
Average Price: Modest
Area: North Dallas
Address: 5850 LBJ Freeway
Dallas, TX 75230
Phone: (469) 804-5353

#467
Erdos At Home
Category: Furniture Stores, Mattresses
Average Price: Expensive
Area: Uptown
Address: 4531 Mckinney Ave
Dallas, TX 75205
Phone: (214) 484-5110

#468
Balani Custom Clothiers
Category: Men's Clothing, Bespoke Clothing
Average Price: Exclusive
Area: West End, Downtown
Address: 701 Commerce St
Dallas, TX 75202
Phone: (214) 646-8587

#469
99 Cents Only Stores
Category: Discount Store, Party Supplies
Average Price: Inexpensive
Area: East Dallas
Address: 4500 Live Oak St
Dallas, TX 75204
Phone: (214) 370-8796

#470
Jonathan Adler
Category: Home Decor
Average Price: Modest
Area: Uptown
Address: 4525 Mckinney Ave
Dallas, TX 75205
Phone: (214) 484-9726

#471
Payless Shoesource
Category: Shoe Stores, Accessories
Average Price: Modest
Area: East Dallas
Address: 2415 N Haskell Ave
Dallas, TX 75204
Phone: (214) 828-0062

#472
Trader Joe's
Category: Grocery
Average Price: Modest
Area: Uptown
Address: 4525 Cole Ave
Dallas, TX 75205
Phone: (214) 599-2155

#473
Movie Trading Company
Category: Videos & Video Game Rental
Average Price: Modest
Area: Upper Greenville
Address: 5809 Greenville Ave
Dallas, TX 75206
Phone: (214) 361-8287

#474
Big Lots - Dallas
Category: Department Stores, Furniture
Stores, Home Decor
Average Price: Modest
Area: North Dallas
Address: 3610 Forest Ln
Dallas, TX 75234
Phone: (214) 350-6419

#475
Target
Category: Department Stores
Average Price: Modest
Area: East Dallas
Address: 2417 N Haskell Ave
Dallas, TX 75204
Phone: (214) 826-0331

#476
Diamond Exchange Dallas
Category: Jewelry
Average Price: Modest
Area: North Dallas
Address: 5757 Alpha Rd
Dallas, TX 75240
Phone: (214) 755-1806

#477
Bebe
Category: Women's Clothing,
Accessories, Shoe Stores
Average Price: Exclusive
Area: North Dallas
Address: 8687 N Central Expy , Ste 624
Dallas, TX 75225
Phone: (214) 365-9400

#478
Rack Room Shoes
Category: Shoe Stores
Average Price: Modest
Area: Addison
Address: 5301 Belt Line Rd
Dallas, TX 75254
Phone: (972) 385-8329

#479
The Diamond Broker
Category: Jewelry, Watches
Average Price: Modest
Area: North Dallas
Address: 11930 Preston Rd
Dallas, TX 75230
Phone: (972) 490-6060

#480
Lane Bryant
Category: Accessories, Women's Clothing
Average Price: Expensive
Area: Victory Park
Address: Park Lane Ctr
Dallas, TX 75219
Phone: (214) 234-0041

#481
Express
Category: Accessories, Men's Clothing
Average Price: Modest
Area: North Dallas
Address: 620 Northpark Ctr
Dallas, TX 75225
Phone: (214) 373-7523

#482
EV's Thrift Store
Category: Thrift Stores
Average Price: Modest
Area: East Dallas
Address: 4307 Willow St
Dallas, TX 75226
Phone: (214) 707-0078

#483
JOURNEYS
Category: Shoe Stores
Average Price: Modest
Area: North Dallas
Address: 8687 N Central Expy
Dallas, TX 75225
Phone: (214) 363-4920

#484
Security Self Storage
Category: Self Storage,
RV Parks, Packing Supplies
Average Price: Modest
Area: North Dallas
Address: 3334 Forest Ln
Dallas, TX 75234
Phone: (972) 590-6841

#485
Big Lots - Farmers Branch
Category: Department Stores
Average Price: Inexpensive
Area: Farmer's Branch
Address: 2865 Valley View Ln Farmers
Branch, TX 75234
Phone: (972) 484-4821

#486
Edo Popken
Category: Men's Clothing
Average Price: Modest
Area: Design District
Address: 1523 Dragon St
Dallas, TX 75207
Phone: (214) 749-0200

#487
Motek Diamonds By IDC
Category: Jewelry, Wholesalers
Average Price: Inexpensive
Area: North Dallas
Address: 5580 Lyndon B Johnson
Fwy Dallas, TX 75240
Phone: (972) 233-6708

#488
Shai Gut Inc
Category: Jewelry
Average Price: Exclusive
Area: North Dallas
Address: 12900 Preston Rd
Dallas, TX 75230
Phone: (972) 980-0608

#489
REI
Category: Sports Wear, Outdoor Gear, Bikes
Average Price: Expensive
Area: Lake Highlands
Address: 5929 E Northwest Hwy
Dallas, TX 75231
Phone: (800) 426-4840

#490
Gamestop
Category: Electronics, Videos &
Video Game Rental
Average Price: Modest
Area: North Dallas
Address: 3450 Webb Chapel Extension
Dallas, TX 75220
Phone: (214) 366-2361

#491
Old Navy
Category: Department Stores
Average Price: Modest
Area: Lake Highlands
Address: 8170 Park Ln
Dallas, TX 75231
Phone: (214) 360-7715

#492
Pac Sun
Category: Women's Clothing, Men's Clothing
Average Price: Modest
Area: North Dallas
Address: 13350 Dallas Pkwy
Dallas, TX 75240
Phone: (972) 661-0782

#493
Foot Locker
Category: Shoe Stores
Average Price: Modest
Area: North Dallas
Address: 11719 Webb Chapel Rd
Dallas, TX 75229
Phone: (972) 243-8920

#494
Tony's Neighborhood Store
Category: Convenience Stores
Average Price: Inexpensive
Area: East Dallas
Address: 820 North Fitzhugh Ave
Dallas, TX 75246
Phone: (469) 828-1409

#495
Tod's North Park
Category: Shoe Stores, Leather Goods
Average Price: Modest
Area: North Dallas
Address: 8687 N Central Expy
Dallas, TX 75225
Phone: (214) 363-6600

#496
Bakers Shoes
Category: Shoe Stores
Average Price: Modest
Area: North Dallas
Address: 8687 N Central Expy
Dallas, TX 75225
Phone: (214) 265-7220

#497
Zsofia's Fine Lingerie
Category: Lingerie
Average Price: Modest
Area: Design District
Address: 1130 Dragon St
Dallas, TX 75207
Phone: (214) 770-7696

#498
Brooks Brothers
Category: Men's Clothing, Women's Clothing
Average Price: Expensive
Area: Uptown
Address: 3636 Mckinney Avenue
Dallas, TX 75204
Phone: (214) 520-8854

#499
Plato's Closet
Category: Used, Vintage & Consignment
Average Price: Inexpensive
Area: Northeast Dallas
Address: 8430 Abrams Rd
Dallas, TX 75243
Phone: (214) 342-2204

#500
Sam's Club
Category: Department Stores
Average Price: Modest
Area: North Dallas
Address: 4062 Lyndon B Johnson Fwy
Dallas, TX 75241
Phone: (972) 934-9274

Made in the USA
Columbia, SC
01 August 2021